T0327881

Dreamy Anime Hair

30+ cute & easy styles from the world's most beloved anime characters

Mei Yan

Illustrations by

EPIC INK

CONTENTS

Intermediate

Advanced

INTRODUCTION

Writing *Dreamy Anime Hair* has been an absolute dream come true. It's been a true passion project, lovingly created over a year and a half of hard work between myself and every wonderful person on this team. I feel both incredibly lucky and honored to be creating work for readers to enjoy.

I've been creating videos on YouTube for over eight years now on my channel Mei Yan, previously known as Princess Mei. I started my journey in hair content creation with my iconic pink hair, which you can still see on the very first video that I uploaded! I've maintained versions of colored hair for over a decade, featuring all colors of the rainbow (and sometimes multiple colors). I've uploaded videos spanning hair topics, from styling tutorials and hair care routines to educational content explaining color corrections and more. Some of my favorite videos have been trips to my beloved hair salon in Los Angeles, California, Level 1 Studio, where I've done hair color transformations of all kinds. Some of these looks have taken up to twelve hours to accomplish—but it has always been worth it! Hair has always been my ultimate expression of self, and I've had the most fun creating hair-related content.

My anime-inspired hairstyle tutorials have become some of my most popular work. The concept of the series started with the idea to tap into the endless wealth of inspiration that I gained as a child from watching my favorite anime series. When I was growing up as a first-generation Chinese-American girl in the '90s, it was incredibly difficult to find relatable content and Asian media.

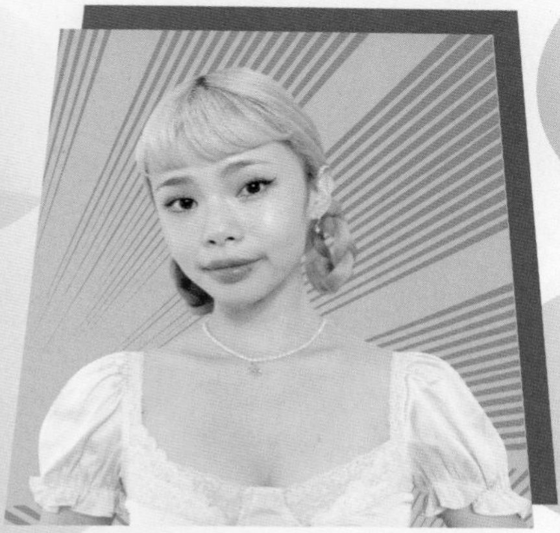

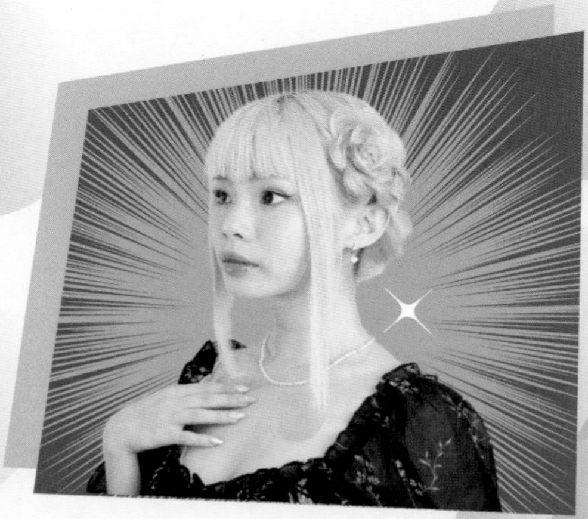

The world of anime was first introduced to me by older relatives, who would help me search for laughably poor-quality episodes of our favorite series on the internet. Despite the struggles of accessibility, I was still instantly sucked into the expansive fantasy worlds of magical powers and compelling heroines.

I began my anime style journey on YouTube by recreating iconic hairstyles from 1990s and early 2000s anime, including a few personal favorite looks from series such as *Cardcaptor Sakura* and *Sailor Moon*. Once I began the series, I received nonstop requests from viewers around the world to cover more and more of their favorite characters. I've compiled a great list of them over the years and created some of them for you in this book! A few styles have already been showcased on my YouTube channel, but I'm bringing them to you again in this book with new techniques and a different spin, to make them either more character accurate or easier to recreate.

I believe hair is the greatest accessory and form of self-expression that most of us have at our disposal. Style and fashion are wonderful when accessible, and all hairstyling needs is just a bit of practice and imagination. I hope that this book inspires you to form a closer bond with your hair, and that it serves as not just a guide but also a source of encouragement for you to get creative. Change the steps of a tutorial along the way, experiment with your own ideas, and add your own sense of style with your favorite accessories.

Most importantly, tap into all the childlike wonder and inspiration you find in the world, and have fun with it!

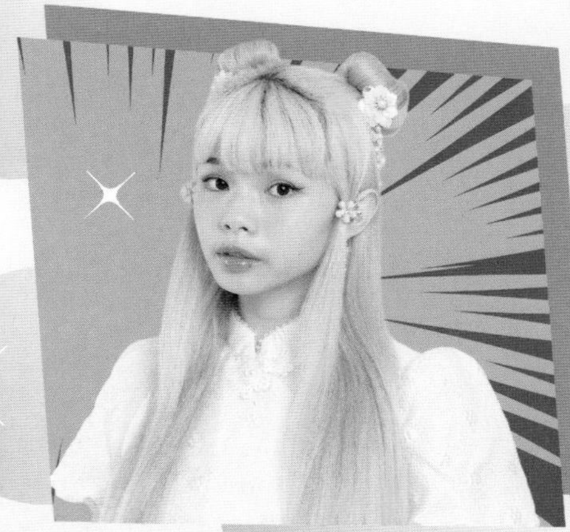

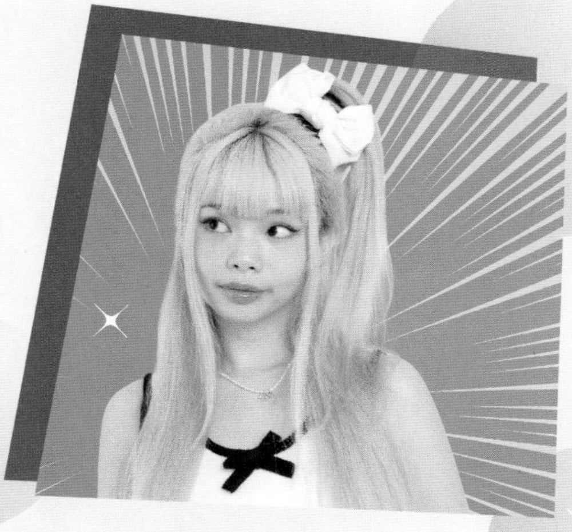

RECOMMENDED PRODUCTS AND TOOLS

Straightening Iron

When choosing your tools, it's incredibly important to familiarize yourself with what's available on the market. There are three common types of materials for heat-styling tools: tourmaline, ceramic, and titanium. Each material has a different heat threshold, so your heat-styling tools should be purchased according to your hair type.

Curling Iron

As with the straightening iron, there are many options, so you should purchase what's best for your hair type. For example, for my naturally straight, thick, and coarse Asian hair, I like to use ceramic heat-styling tools with an ion generator feature to reduce frizz.

Heat Protection

It goes without saying, but always use heat protection to keep your hair safe when styling with heated tools like straightening irons or curling irons. Heat protection products are formulated to coat the hair during styling to prevent heat damage, and some products even help hair stay soft and bouncy afterward, making them perfect for creating luscious curls.

Hairbrush

I use two different types of hairbrushes depending on what style I want to achieve. For most looks, I use a detangling hairbrush with soft and malleable bristles to reduce breakage and damage when brushing my hair. For sleek and tidy updos, I use a boar-bristle brush to smooth all flyaways into place.

Clip-in Hair Extensions

Since some anime hairstyles can be more colorful and voluminous than your average look, I like to keep different types of hair extensions on hand. I have an entire set of human hair extensions, as well as several sets of 1-inch hair extensions in different colors, because they're a great way to add a pop of color when needed.

BASIC TECHNIQUES

Nonslip Ponytail

While the ponytail is the most standard technique used for creating hairstyles, this nonslip ponytail is an elevated technique to keep all ponytails perky throughout the day.

Tools: Elastics, Boar-bristle hairbrush, Hair spray

1 Starting at the temples as a guideline, gather one-fourth of hair into a small high ponytail.

2 Spray with hair spray and brush back with a boar-bristle hairbrush to smooth down flyaways.

3 Use two small elastic hair ties to keep this small ponytail in place. It's important to use two hair ties to ensure a secure hold.

4 Gather the rest of the hair up to meet the small high ponytail.

5 Brush to smooth out and use two more hair ties for an ultra-secure hold.

Three-strand Braid

The three-strand braid is one of the basic techniques used for hairstyling. When you master these basic techniques, you can apply them in different and unexpected ways to create even the most intricate-looking hairstyles.

Tools: Elastics

1 Take a section of hair and split it into three equal sections.

2 Think of the hair as three sections: the left, the middle, and the right. Take the right section and pass it over the middle section.

3 Take the left section and pass it over the middle section.

4 Repeat steps 2 and 3 as many times as necessary before securing the braid with an elastic.

Rope Braid

The rope braid isn't an often-used braiding technique, but it's incredibly easy to learn. By familiarizing yourself with more basic techniques, you can better understand the way hair works and how you can begin to create more intricate hairstyles.

Tools: Elastics

1 Separate a portion of hair into two even sections.

2 Twist both individual sections in the same direction. The tighter the twist, the more taut and secure the rope braid will be.

3 Now twist the sections of hair together in the opposite direction. The twisting motion in the opposite direction will keep the hair secured in place, just like how a rope is made.

4 Secure with an elastic.

French Braid

A French braid is another basic technique that's a great skill for all beginners to know before creating more intricate hairstyles. It's also a technique that looks adorable on its own!

Tools: Elastics

1 Start by separating a section of hair into three parts. As with a regular three-strand braid, think of the hair as three sections: the left, the middle, and the right.

2 Begin braiding the hair by passing the left strand over the middle strand.

3 Pass the right strand over the middle strand.

4 Incorporate a small section of hair into the left strand before passing it over the middle strand once again.

5 Incorporate a small section of hair into the right strand before passing it over the middle strand.

6 Continue braiding the hair by adding a small section of hair to the side strands before passing each one over the middle strand.

7 You can only apply this technique directly on the head, so continue French braiding down to the nape of the neck.

8 Finish off with a regular three-strand braid technique and tie with an elastic to complete the braid.

Dutch Braid

Also known as an inverted French braid, the Dutch braid is my personal favorite type of braid. As shown in the previous tutorial, the French braid weaves the hair on top of itself. The Dutch braid instead weaves the hair under itself, so that the braid has a 3D effect sitting on top of the head.

Tools: Elastics

1 Begin by separating a section of hair into three parts. As with a regular three-strand braid, think of the hair as three sections: the left, the middle, and the right.

2 Start braiding the hair by passing the right strand underneath the middle strand.

3 Pass the left strand underneath the middle strand.

4 Incorporate a small section of hair into the right strand.

5 Pass it underneath the middle strand once again.

6 Incorporate a small section of hair into the left strand.

7 Pass it underneath the middle strand.

8 Continue braiding the hair by adding a small section of hair to the side strands before passing each one underneath the middle strand. You can only apply this technique directly on the head, so continue Dutch braiding down to the nape of the neck.

9 Finish off with a regular three-strand braid technique and tie with an elastic to complete the braid.

Curling Technique

While there are many ways to curl hair, this is personally my favorite way to create long-lasting voluminous curls. Before starting, be sure to familiarize yourself with the different types of curling irons on the market. I prefer to use a curling wand versus a curling iron because I personally feel that it's easier to control. My go-to curling wand has a detachable barrel so that I can swap out different sizes to create different types of curls. The smaller the barrel size, the tighter the curl will be. Alternatively, the larger the barrel size, the looser the curls will be. I prefer to use a 2-inch-barrel for the perfect soft wave.

Tools: Detangling hairbrush, Heat protection spray, Curling wand or curling iron, Bobby pins, Heat protection glove, Wide-tooth comb (optional)

1 Split the hair in half and thoroughly brush through to detangle all knots.

2 Apply an ample amount of heat protection product throughout the hair.

3 Working in 1-inch sections, wrap the hair around the barrel of the curling wand in the direction away from your face, using the hand wearing the heat protection glove. Let the hair heat thoroughly to set the curl. The amount of time needed to heat the curl will vary with different hair types and textures, so experiment until you find your perfect timing.

4 Release the curl from the barrel and gently recoil the curl.

5 Pin against the head. This step lets the curl cool while retaining its shape. The result is ultra-long-lasting and bouncy curls.

6 Repeat steps 3–5 until all sections of hair are curled. Allow the hair to completely cool down before releasing all curls.

7 Gently brush the curls out with either a wide-tooth comb or your fingers.

CHARACTER KEY

EASY

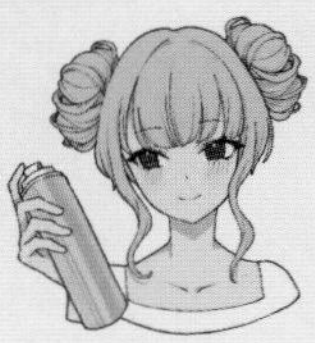

Himiko Toga

Himiko Toga is a member of the League of Villains in *My Hero Academia*, and her superpower (known as a *quirk* in the series) allows her to transform into the physical form of another person by ingesting their blood.

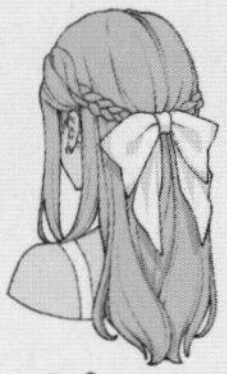

Yuuki Asuna

Yuuki Asuna is one of the female leads in the anime, *Sword Art Online*. Her skills with the rapier earned her the nickname "The Flash", and she has been the leader of many groups in the series.

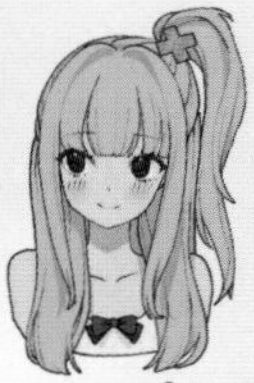

Hinamori Amu

Hinamori Amu is the main heroine of the manga and anime, *Shugo Chara*. She is cold and stoic at first, hiding her shyness, but she becomes friendlier after meeting her Guardians.

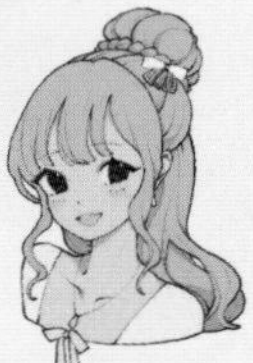

Lacus Clyne

Lacus Clyne is an idol singer in the anime, *Gundam Seed Destiny*. She seems to be naive, but her thoughtful speeches throughout the series reveal a deep and philosophical personality.

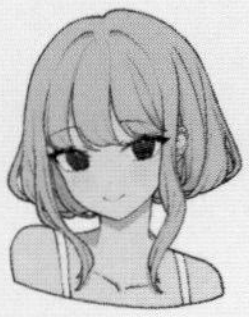

Uraraka

Uraraka is a pro-hero student in Class 1-A at U.A. High School in *My Hero Academia*. Her quirk is Zero Gravity, allowing her to null the effects of gravity on an object of her choosing.

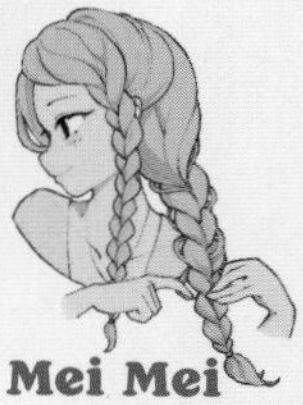

Mei Mei

Mei Mei is a grade 1 jujutsu sorcerer in the manga and anime series, *Jujutsu Kaisen*. She is the only sorcerer who works in exchange for money, and she was once the senpai of Satoru Gojo and Suguru Geto.

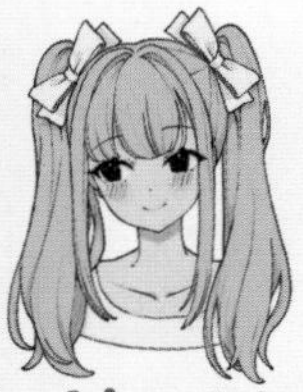

Hoshina Utau

Hoshina Utau is a high school student who became a singing idol in the manga and anime, *Shugo Chara*. She is an independent artist and the main vocalist of the indie band, Black Diamond.

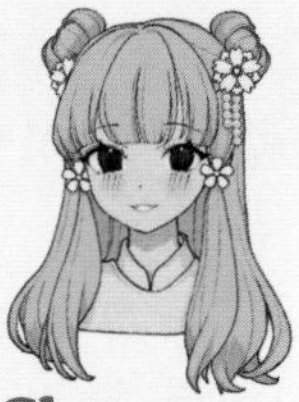

Shampoo

Shampoo is a Chinese Amazon and one of the fiancées of Ranma Saotome in the anime, *Ranma ½*. She first met Ranma when he was disguised as a woman and sought revenge after he defeated her in a public battle.

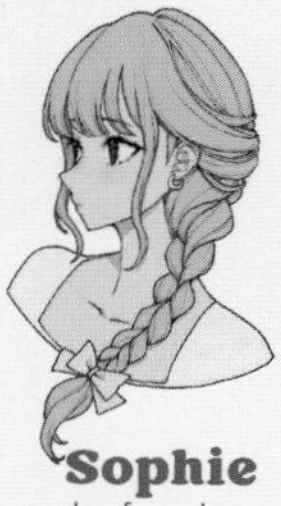

Sophie

Sophie is the female protagonist and heroine of *Howl's Moving Castle*. In the Studio Ghibil film, she goes on an adventure to undo the curse that the Witch of the Waste has placed on her.

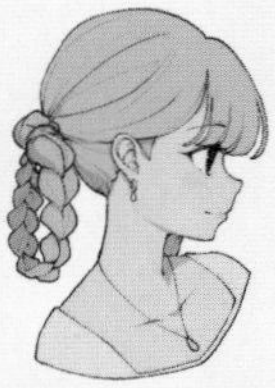

Nurse Joy

Nurse Joy is the shared name of multiple nurses at Pokémon Centers throughout the *Pokémon* games and anime, nursing sick and injured Pokémon back to perfect health.

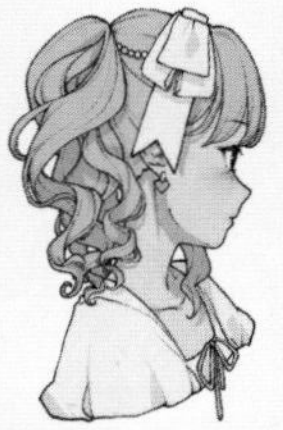

Elizabeth Midford

Elizabeth Midford is the fiancée of Ciel Phantomhive in the manga and anime series, *Black Butler*. She is elegant and graceful, and she is not afraid to wield a sword when necessary.

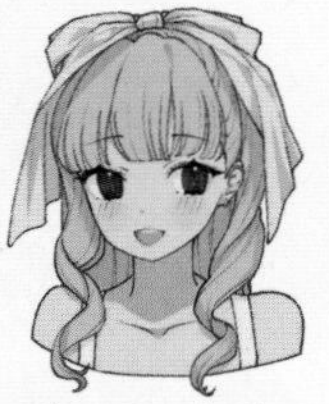

Marie Antoinette

Marie Antoinette, like her historical counterpart, is the queen of France in the 1970s anime, *The Rose of Versailles*. She is known for her beauty, but later becomes a hated figure.

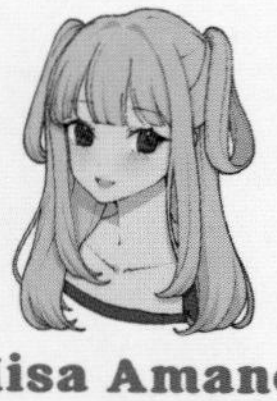

Misa Amane

Misa Amane is a model and actress from the manga and anime series, *Death Note*. She romantically seeks out Kira, the infamous killer in Japan, and supports his cause to "cleanse the world of evil."

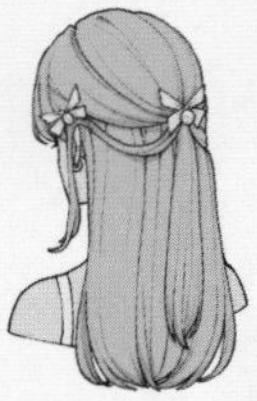

Dawn

Dawn is a Pokémon Coordinator from Twinleaf Town and a former traveling companion of Ash and Brock. The first Pokémon she received from Professor Rowan was Piplup.

INTERMEDIATE

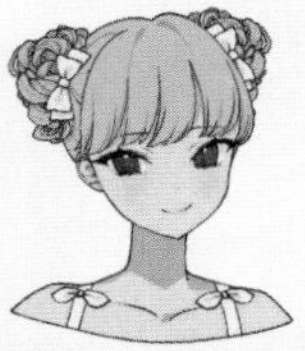

Sakura Miwako

Sakura Miwako is a former student of the Yazawa School in the manga and anime series, *Paradise Kiss*. She is known for unique blend of fashion, part Japanese street wear and part punk rock.

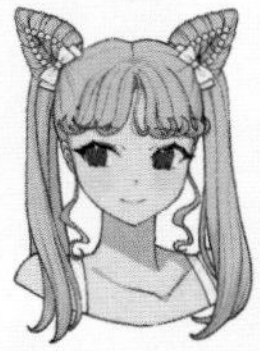

Chibi Usa

Chibi Usa is one of the main characters from the manga and anime series, *Sailor Moon*. Her name translates to "little rabbit." She is the future daughter of Sailor Moon.

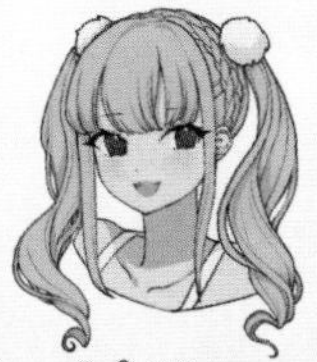

Mitsuki Kouyama

Mitsuki Kouyama is the main protagonist of the manga and anime series, *Full Moon o Sagashite*. Though she has a tumor in her throat, giving her only one year to alive, she has big dreams of becoming a pop singer.

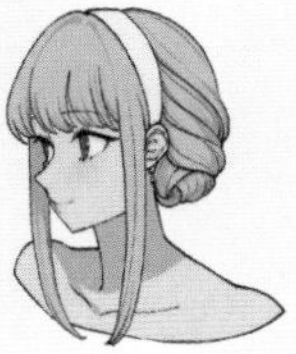

Yor Forger

Yor Forger is one of the protagonists of the manga and anime series, *Spy x Family*. She leads a secret life as a Garden assassin with the code name, Thorn Princess.

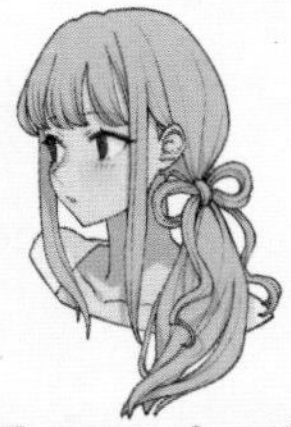

Tsuyu Asui

Tsuyu Asui is a pro-hero student in Class 1-A at U.A. High School in *My Hero Academia* who has a frog-like appearance and abilities. She is also the best friend of Uraraka.

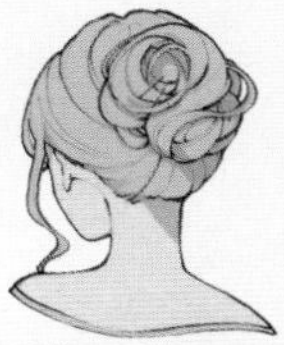

Blue Rose

Blue Rose is a superhero who uses her heroic feats to start her career as a singer in the anime series, *Tiger & Bunny*. She also works as a pianist and singer under her real name.

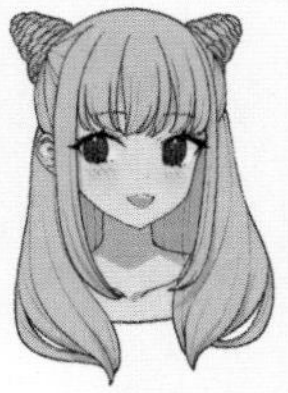

Anya

Anya is the adoptive daughter of Yor Forger and her husband Loid in *Spy x Family*. Formerly Test Subject 007 of an unknown organization, she has telepathic abilities.

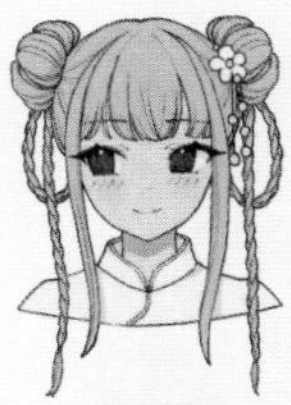

Ran-Mao

Ran-Mao is an assassin in the manga and anime series, *Kuroshitsuji*. She carries two meteor hammers and though she may seem aloof, she is a deceptively skilled fighter.

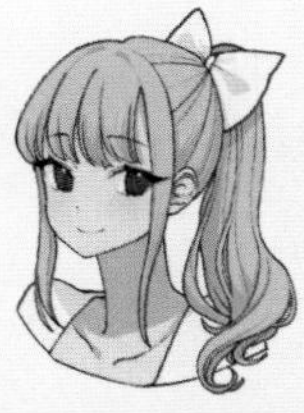

Biscuit Krueger

Biscuit Krueger is a professional Treasure and Double-Star Stone Hunter in the manga and anime series, *Hunter x Hunter*

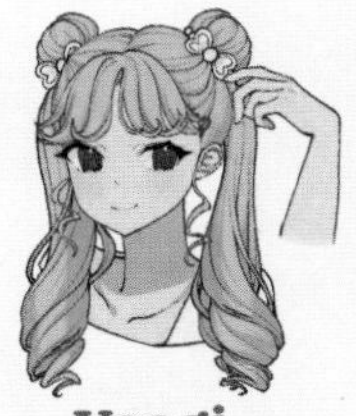

Usagi

Usagi Tsukino is the iconic protagonist and title character of the manga and anime series, *Sailor Moon*. She is the Sailor Guardian of love and justice and the reincarnation of the Moon Princess.

ADVANCED

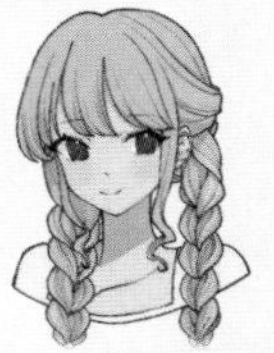

Mitsuri Kanroji

Mitsuri Kanroji from the manga and anime series, *Demon Slayer*, is a member of the Demon Slayer Corps. She has enhanced flexibility and abnormal physical strength.

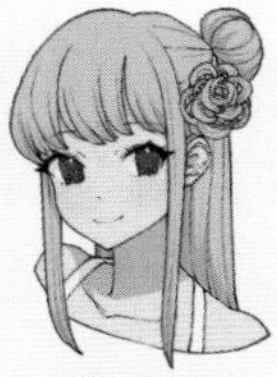

Konan

Konan is an S-ranked ninja in the ninja terrorist group, Akatsuki, in *Naruto*. She was able to combine her origami skills with her chakra, causing her to be greatly feared by her opponents.

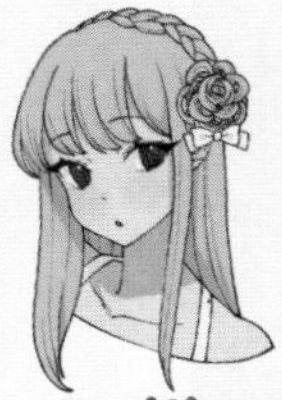

Emilia

Emilia is a candidate to be the forty-second King of the Dragon Kingdom of Luguncia in the manga and anime series, *Re:Zero*. She is half-elf and good-natured.

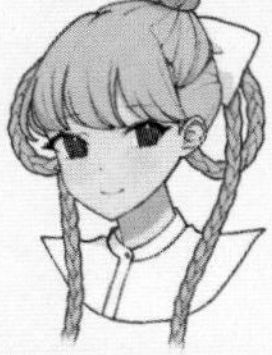

CereCere

CereCere is the Flower Magician of the Dark Moon Circus in the manga and anime series, *Sailor Moon*, and she tends to chase after people who praise her beauty.

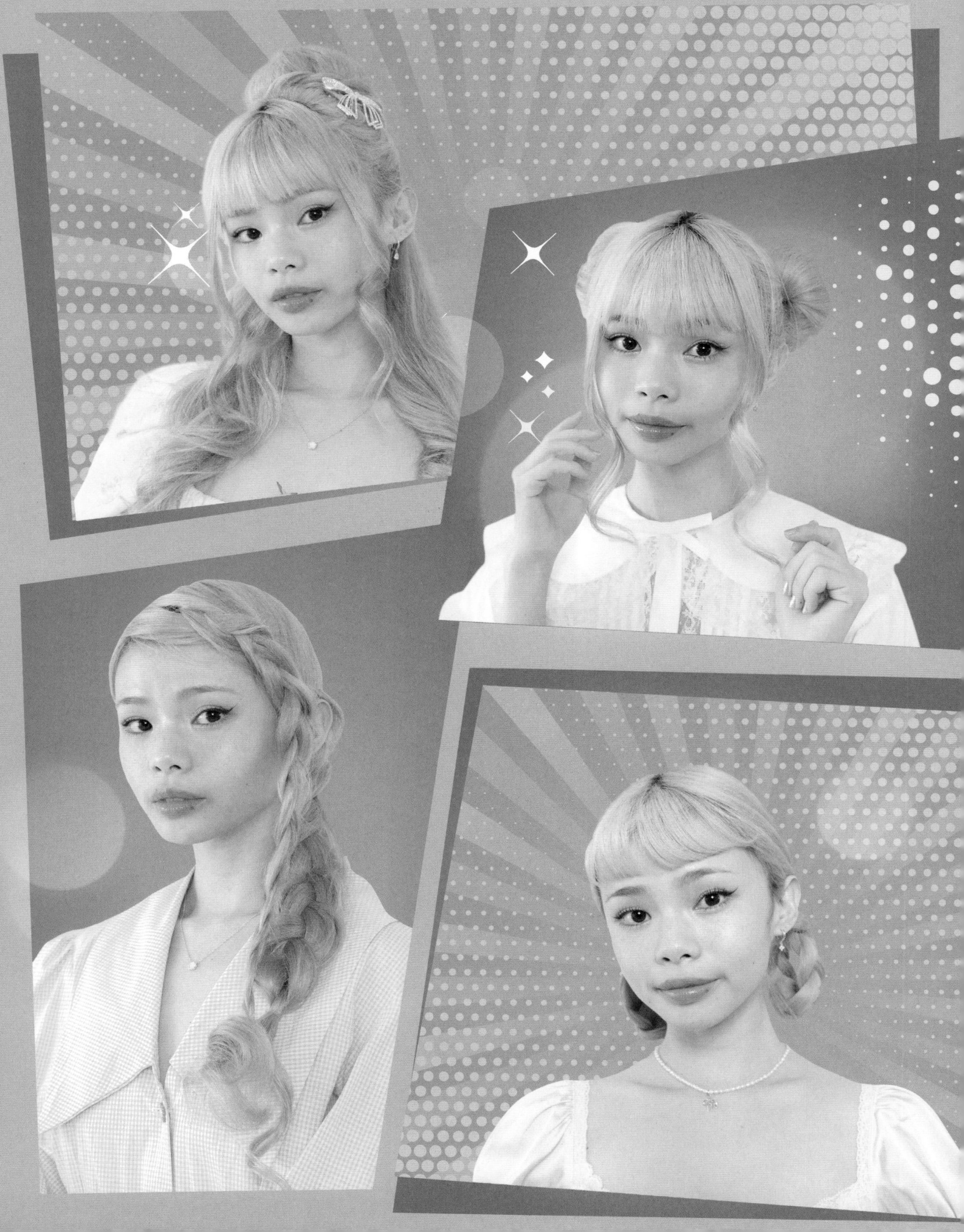

EASY

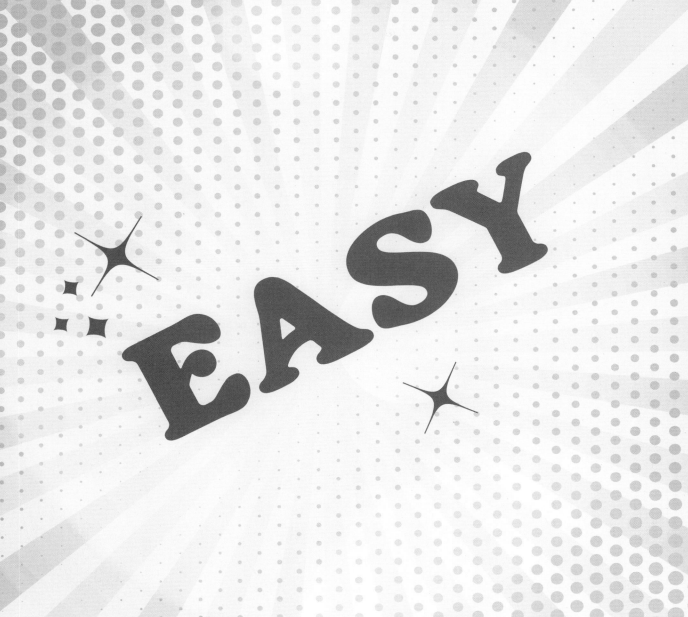

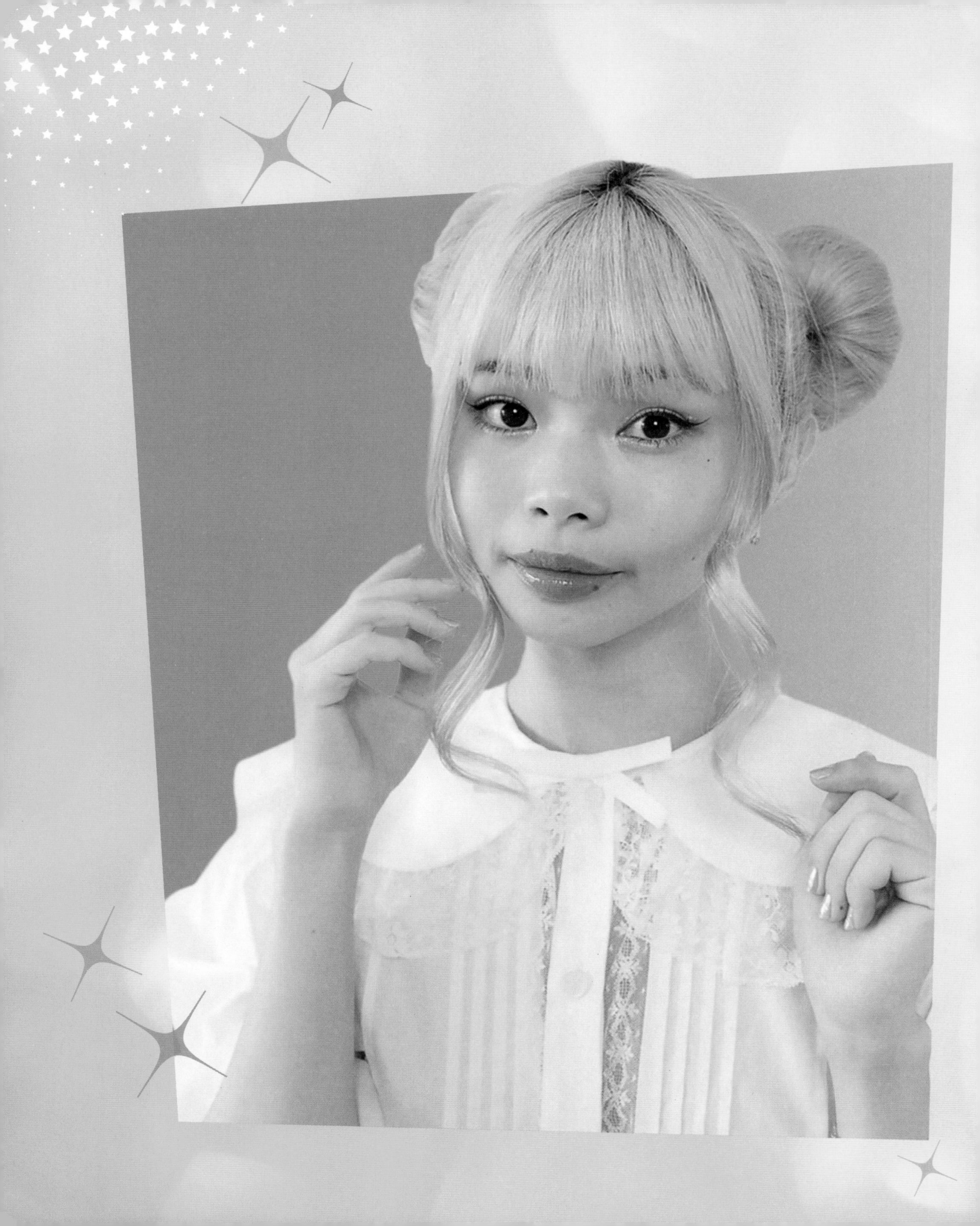

Himiko Toga

My Hero Academia

My Hero Academia is undoubtedly one of the most popular anime series of our generation, with exciting designs and many different types of hairstyles from which to draw inspiration. You'll find a few of them in this book. Himiko Toga wears an ultra-messy and voluminous twin bun hairstyle that perfectly matches her villainess personality. Here's a quick and easy way to achieve a similar style that's a bit more understated, so that it can even be worn as an everyday look.

Tools

Rat-tail comb • Hair spray • Boar-bristle brush • Elastics • Bun maker • Bobby pins

1 Start with curled hair to help add more texture and volume.

2 With a rat-tail comb, split the hair straight down the center.

6 Use a bun maker to roll the hair up into a quick and easy bun, keeping the hair as loose as possible.

7 Secure the bun in place with bobby pins.

3 Split a 1-inch section of hair on each side to frame the face.

4 Gather the hair and pull into a high pigtail on each side.

5 Use hair spray and a boar-bristle brush on the roots to smooth the hair and then tie with two elastics.

8 Loosen the bun with fingers to create a more voluminous and messy look.

9 Lightly hair-spray in place.

Uraraka

My Hero Academia

Uraraka from *My Hero Academia* wears a short, voluminous bob that reflects her bubbly personality. With a few tricks and tips, this hairstyle is perfect for those with longer hair wanting a faux bob without the commitment! I particularly love this hairstyle for warm-weather days, and I can imagine all kinds of adorable looks with different hair accessories! Think floral motif hair clips, delicately tied ribbon bows, and even strands of faux pearls. Short hair may be a simple look, but you can easily add interest with different textures and accessories!

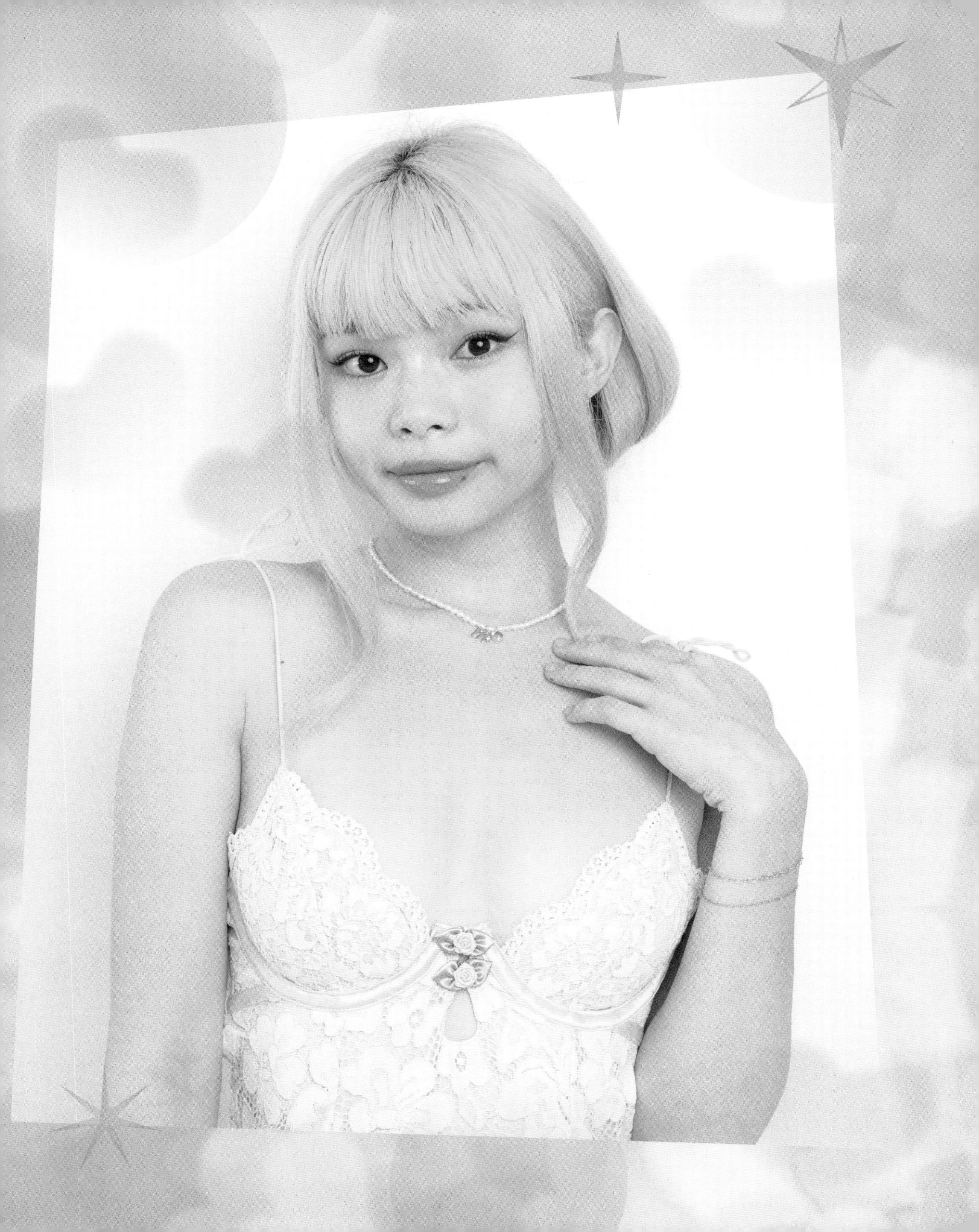

Tools

Rat-tail comb • Bobby pins • Hair spray

1 Start with loosely curled hair.

4 Roll each section of hair underneath until reaching the nape of the neck.

2 Using a rat-tail comb, section off 1-inch sections of hair to frame the face.

3 Split the remaining hair into four sections.

5 Bobby pin each roll into place to create a bubble-shaped faux bob.

6 Hair-spray in place.

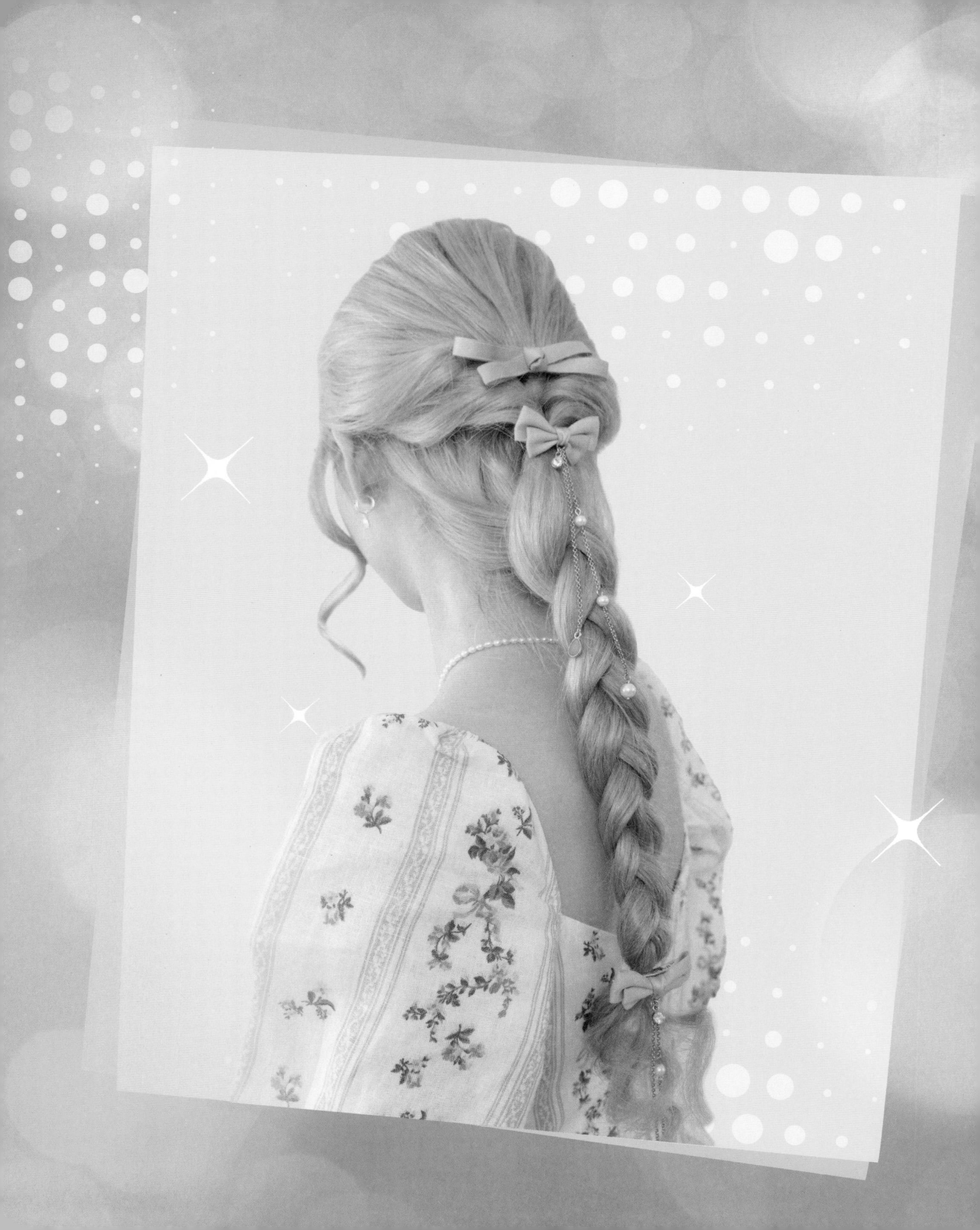

Sophie

Howl's Moving Castle

Studio Ghibli has been a source of inspiration since I was a child, with its stylized films and storytelling, and their movies provided some of my first exposure to animation. *Howl's Moving Castle* is undoubtedly a favorite childhood film for many of us. The heroine, Sophie, wears a simple three-strand braid, but I love to take simple hairstyles and add my own touch to them when bringing them to life. It gives them more magic and personality, and makes them truly unique to me. I encourage you to play with different techniques, even if that means the final product deviates from the original look!

Tools

Elastics • Two hair bows

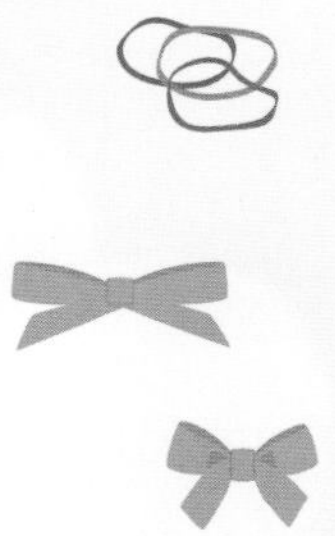

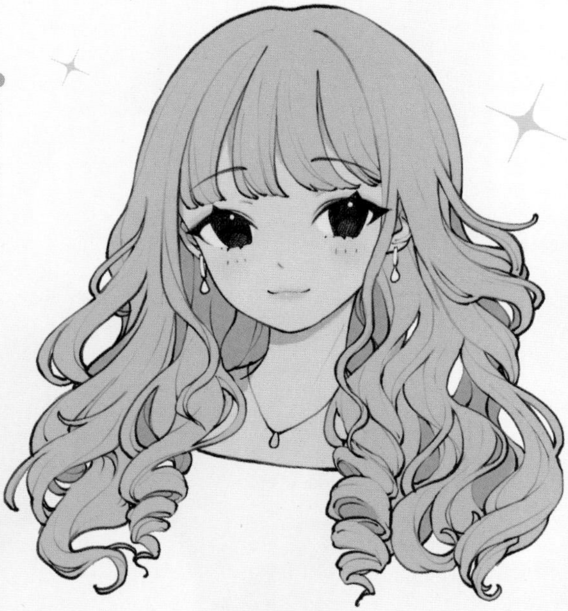

1 Start with curled hair to help add more texture and volume.

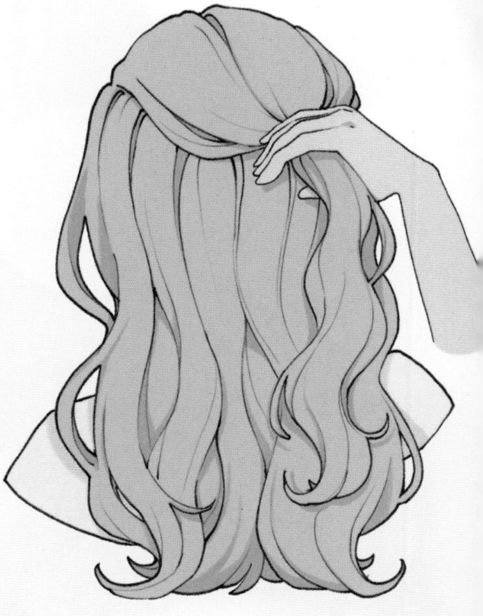

2 Gather the top third section of hair into a loose ponytail and secure with an elastic.

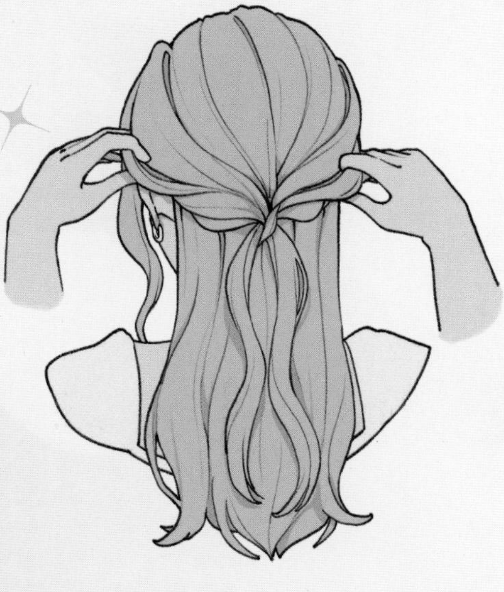

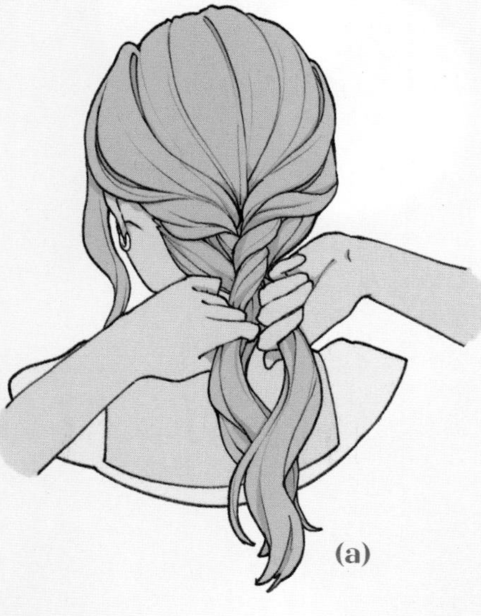

(a)

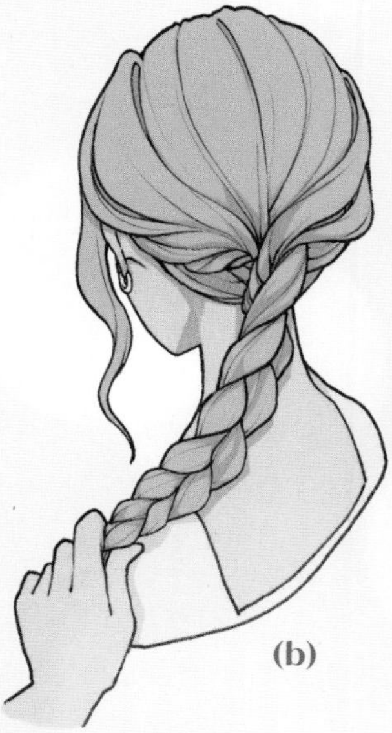

(b)

6 Lightly loosen with fingers for volume. Gather all the hair into a low ponytail and secure with an elastic.

7 Braid into a loose three-strand braid (a) and loosen with fingers for volume, then secure with an elastic (b).

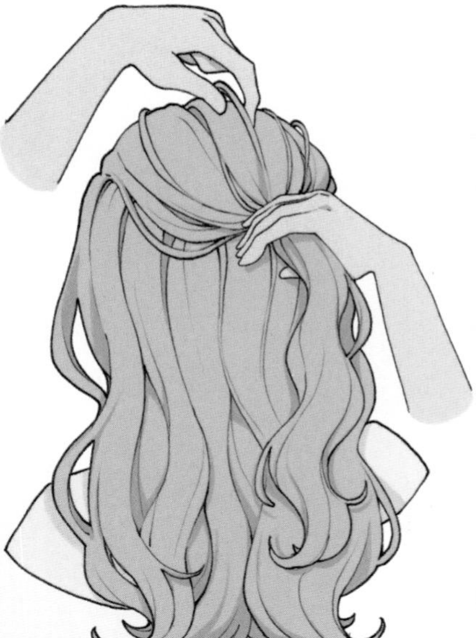

3 Create soft volume by pinching sections of hair to gently loosen the half updo.

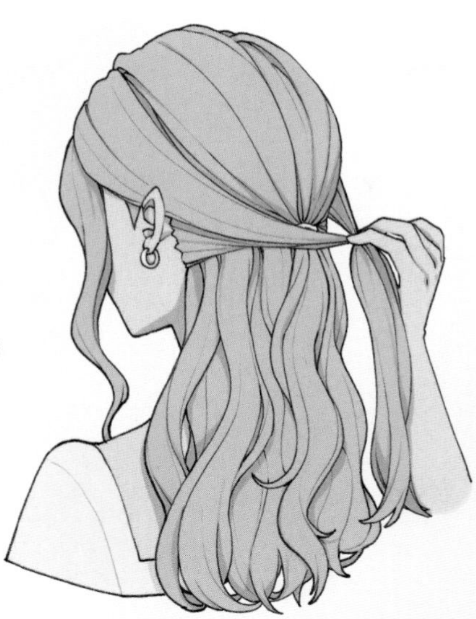

4 Gather the next middle third section of hair and loosely secure with an elastic.

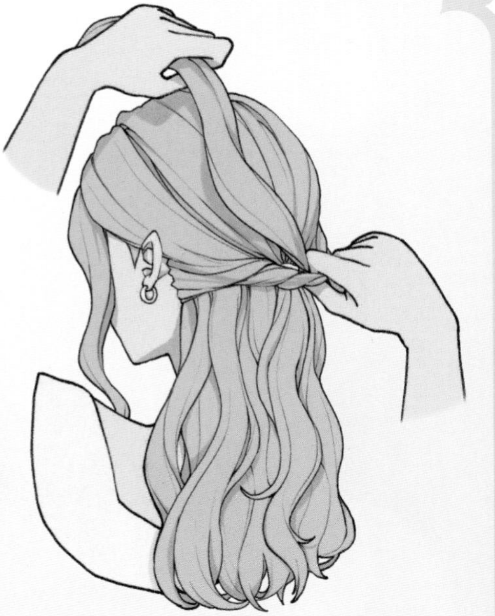

5 Invert the ponytail twice.

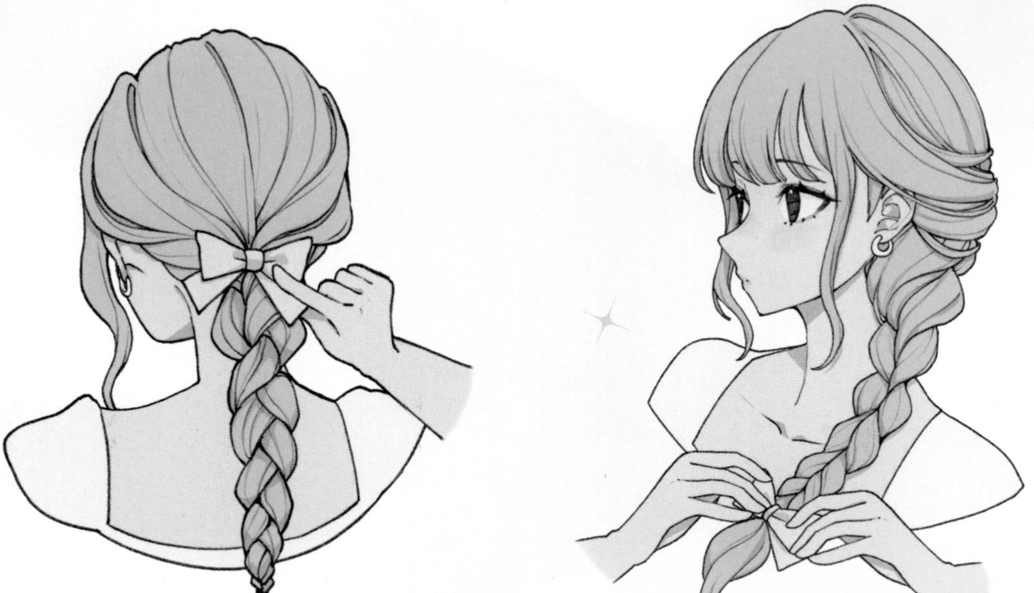

8 Accessorize with hair bows at the top and bottom of the braid.

Misa Amane

Death Note

From one of my favorite series, Misa Amane from *Death Note* is another iconic anime character, well known for her cuteness and gothic style. Misa wears a pair of two small twin tails, but with shorter layers. For those of us who don't want to commit to cutting shorter layers, here's a quick little hack to get a similar look.

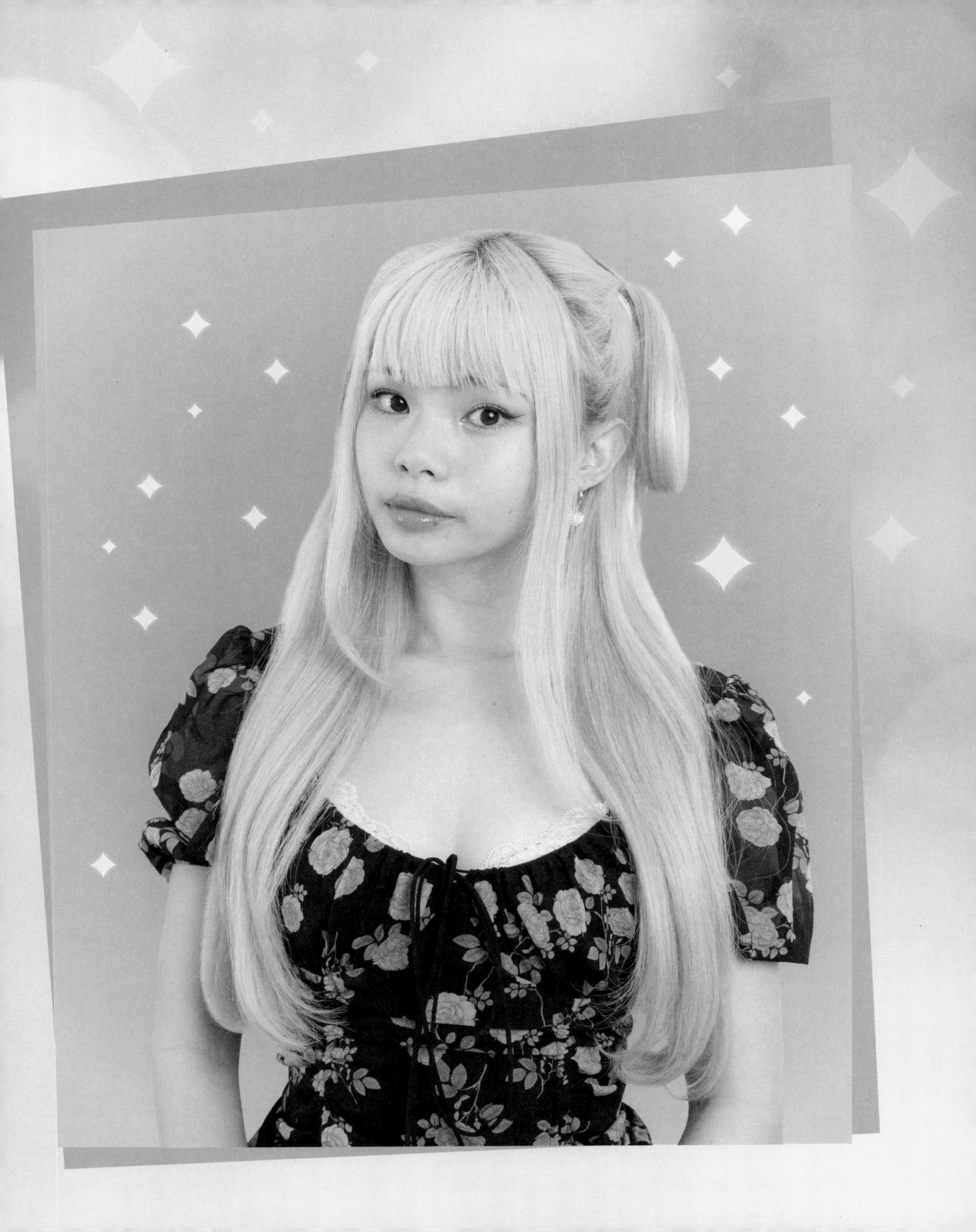

Tools

Rat-tail comb • Elastics
• Straightening iron
• Hair spray

1 Start with straight hair.

2 Using a rat-tail comb, section off 1-inch sections of hair to frame the face.

4 Tie each pigtail into a loose loop.

3 Gather 2-inch sections of hair into two high pigtails and secure with elastics.

5 Gently curl in the ends of the hair with a straightening iron for the finishing touch.

6 Spray with hair spray to make sure your look stays in place.

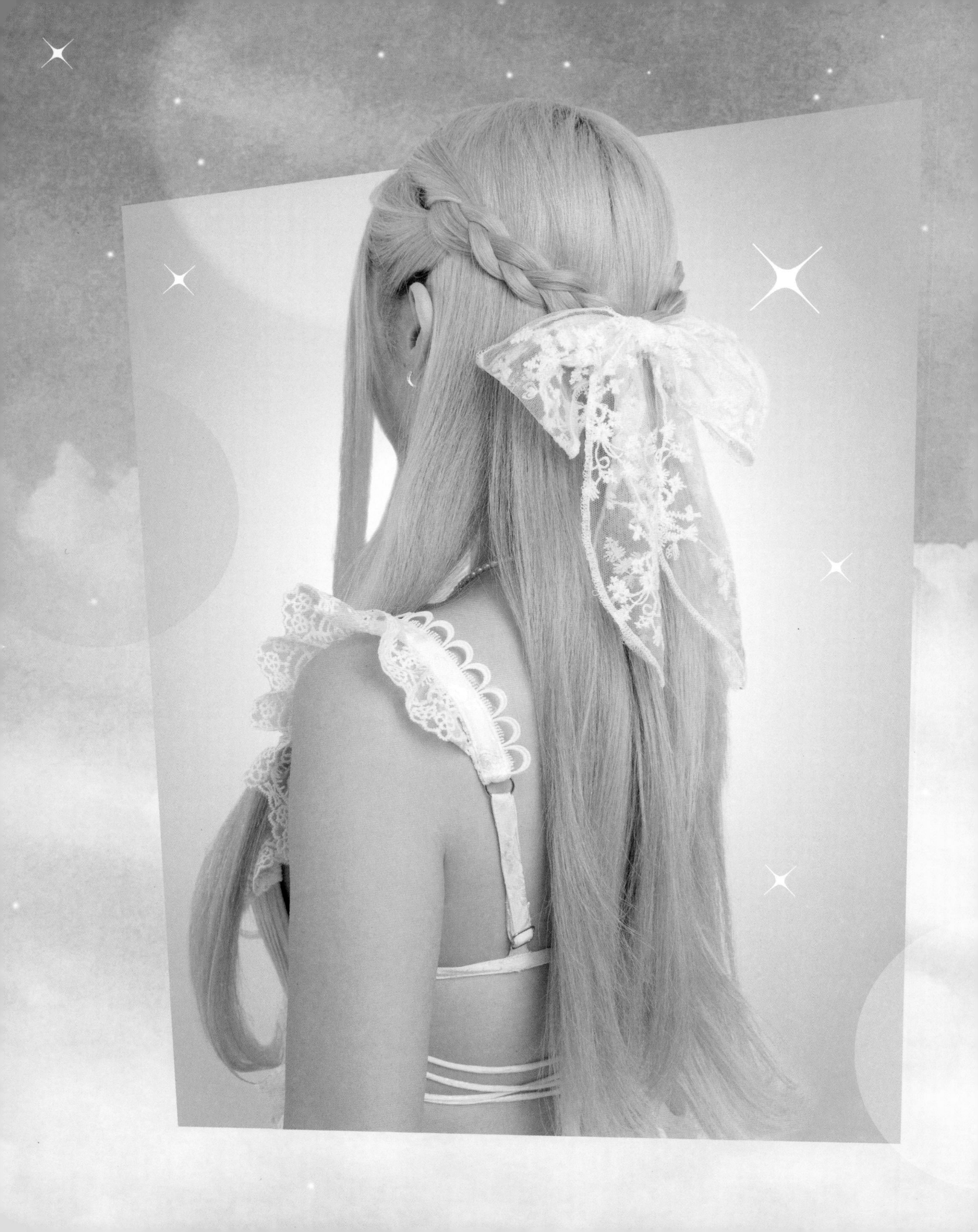

Asuna

Sword Art Online

Asuna from *Sword Art Online* wears one of the cutest and most versatile hairstyles with her thick braided crown. If you're looking for a hairstyle that subtly references anime, then this look is for you. It's perfect for daily wear, or you can dress it up for a special occasion with curls and additional hair accessories.

Tools

Rat-tail comb
• Elastics • White ribbon

1 Start with straight hair.

4 Gently loosen the braids with fingers to add volume.

5 Join both braids in the back and secure with an elastic.

2 Using a rat-tail comb, section off 1-inch sections of hair to frame the face.

3 Gather 2-inch sections of hair above the ear on each side and braid into two three-strand braids.

6 Accessorize with a white ribbon.

Mei Mei

Jujutsu Kaisen

Jujutsu Kaisen is currently one of the most popular anime series and I knew I had to cover some hairstyles from the show in this book. One of my favorite challenges is to take frankly ridiculous anime hairstyles and turn them into something elegant and wearable. When I first met Mei Mei, with one braid down her back and one falling over her face, I couldn't help but laugh at her hair. Challenge accepted.

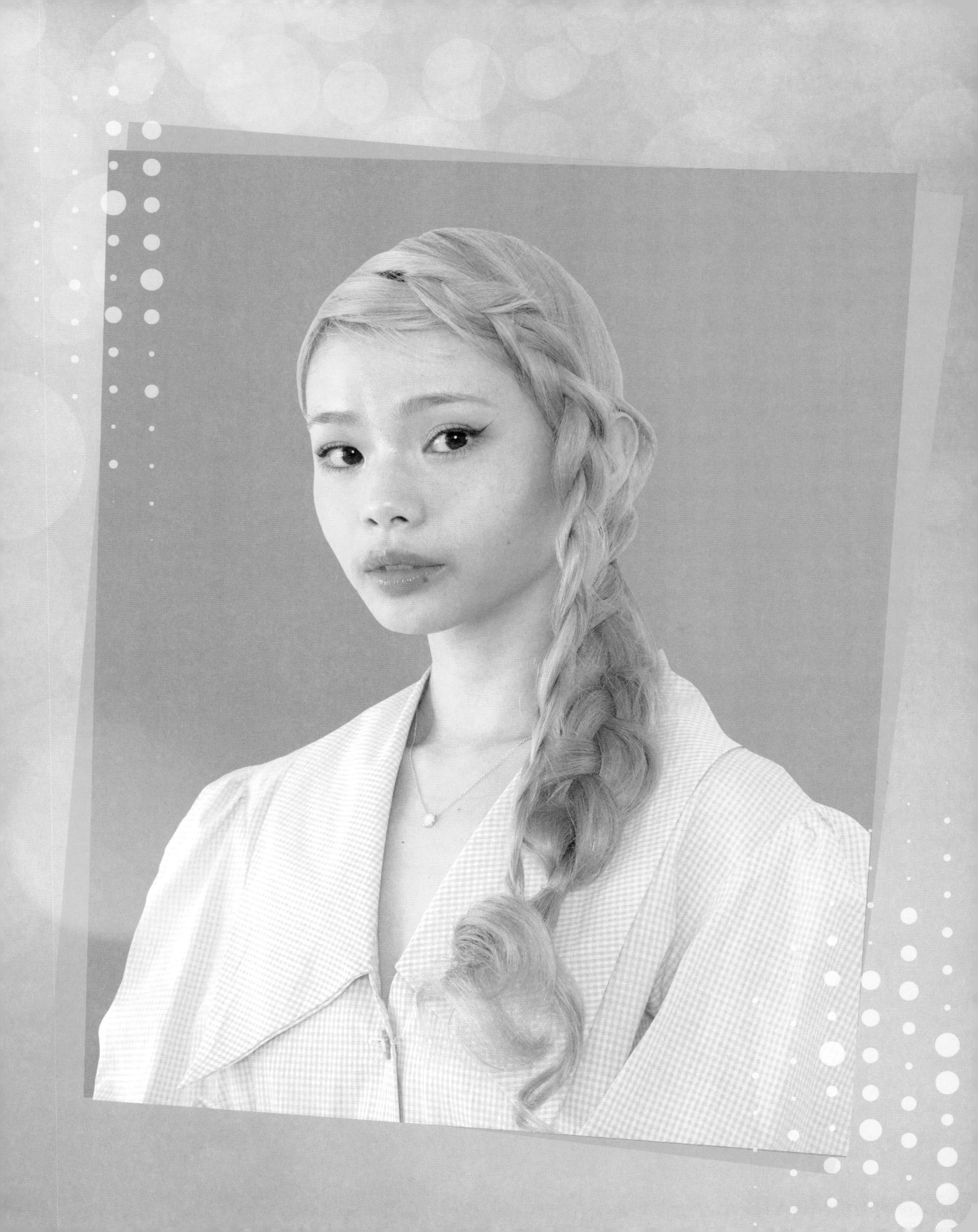

Tools

Elastics

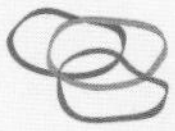

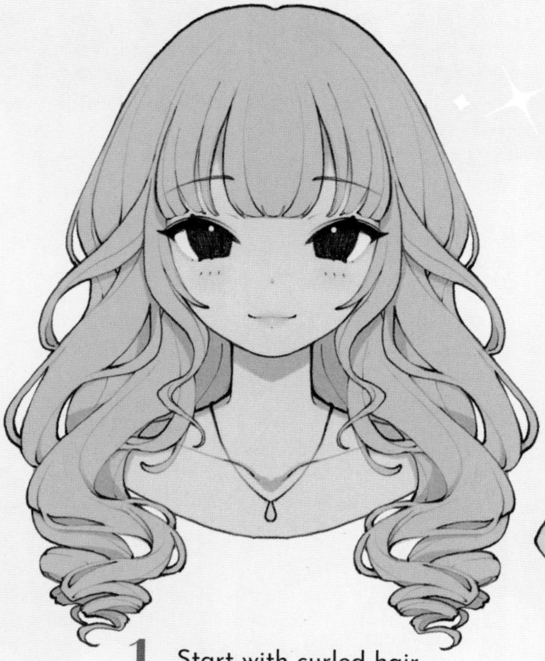

1 Start with curled hair.

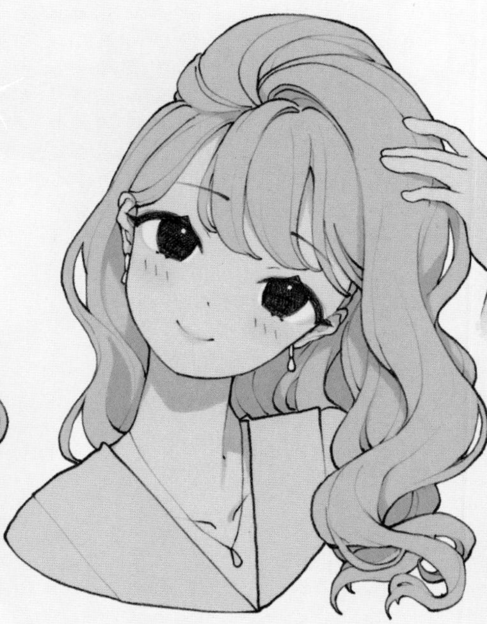

2 Flip one third of hair forward over the left side of the face.

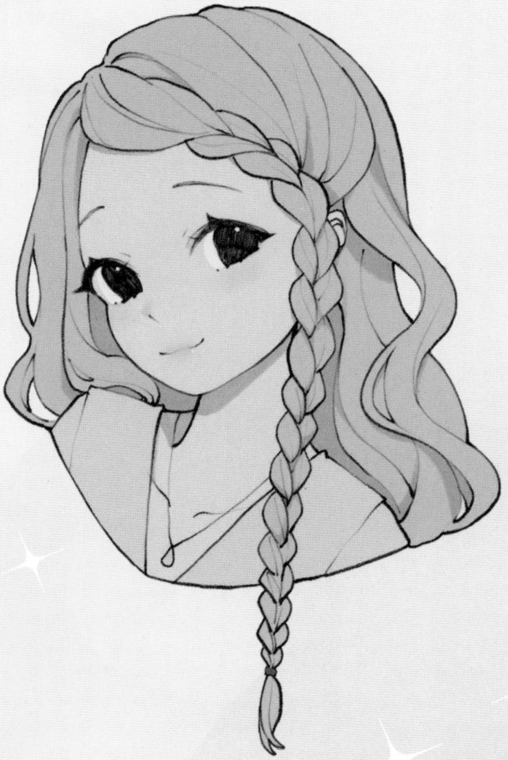

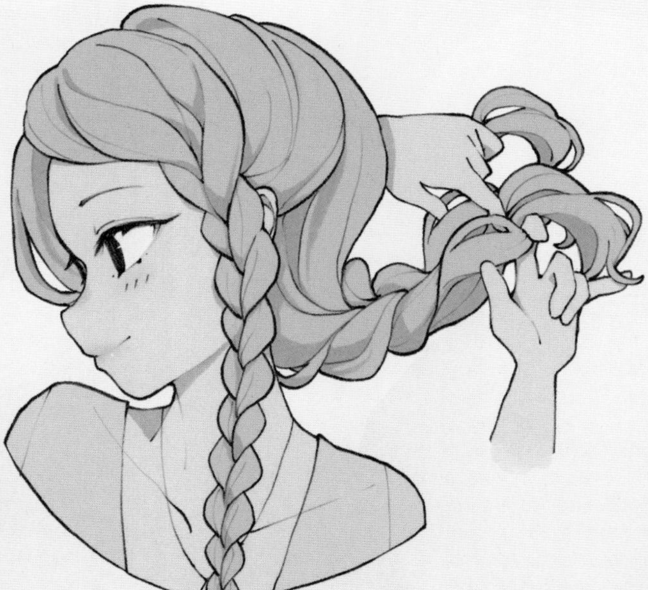

4 Gather the remaining half section of hair from the back and braid into a regular loose, three-strand braid. Secure with an elastic.

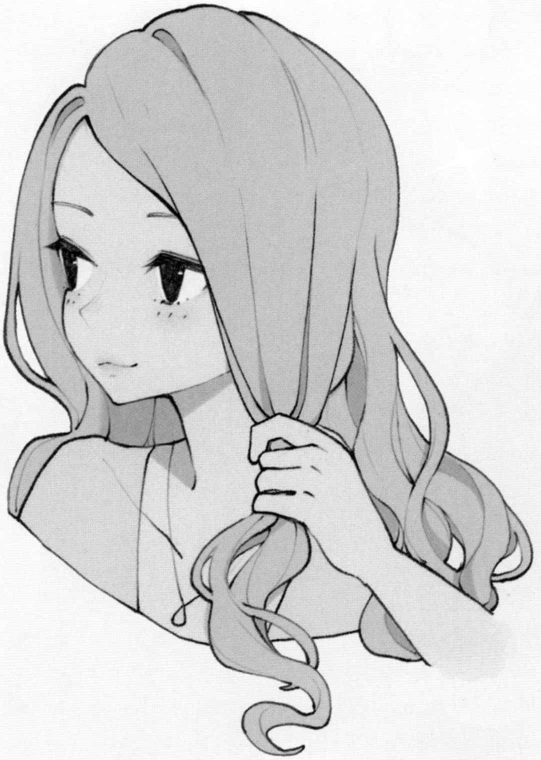

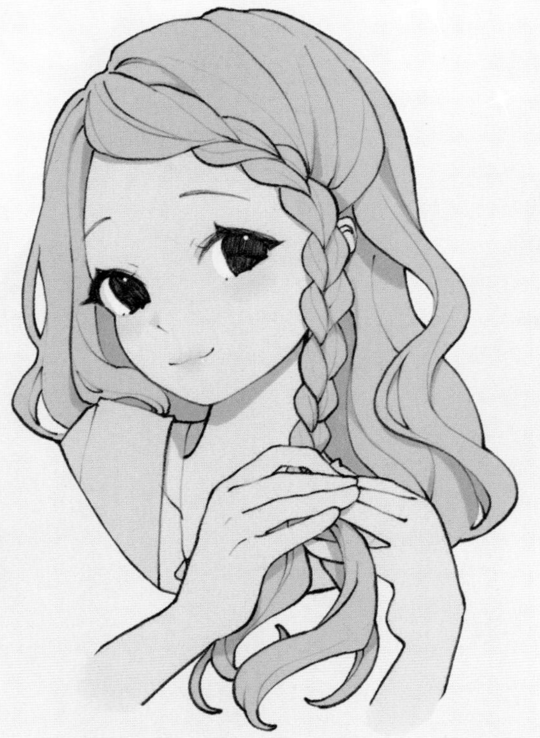

3 Starting with a 1-inch section of hair from the top, braid into a three-strand Dutch braid and secure with an elastic.

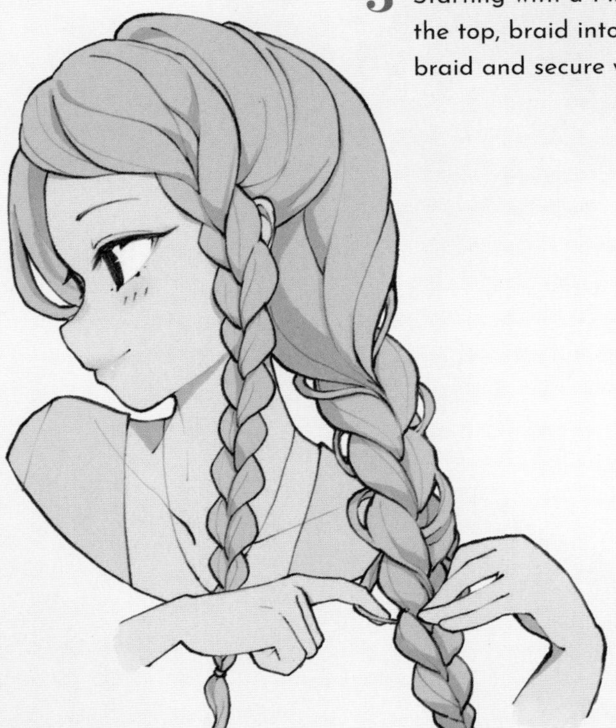

5 Gently loosen both braids by tugging on each side of the braid to give it more volume.

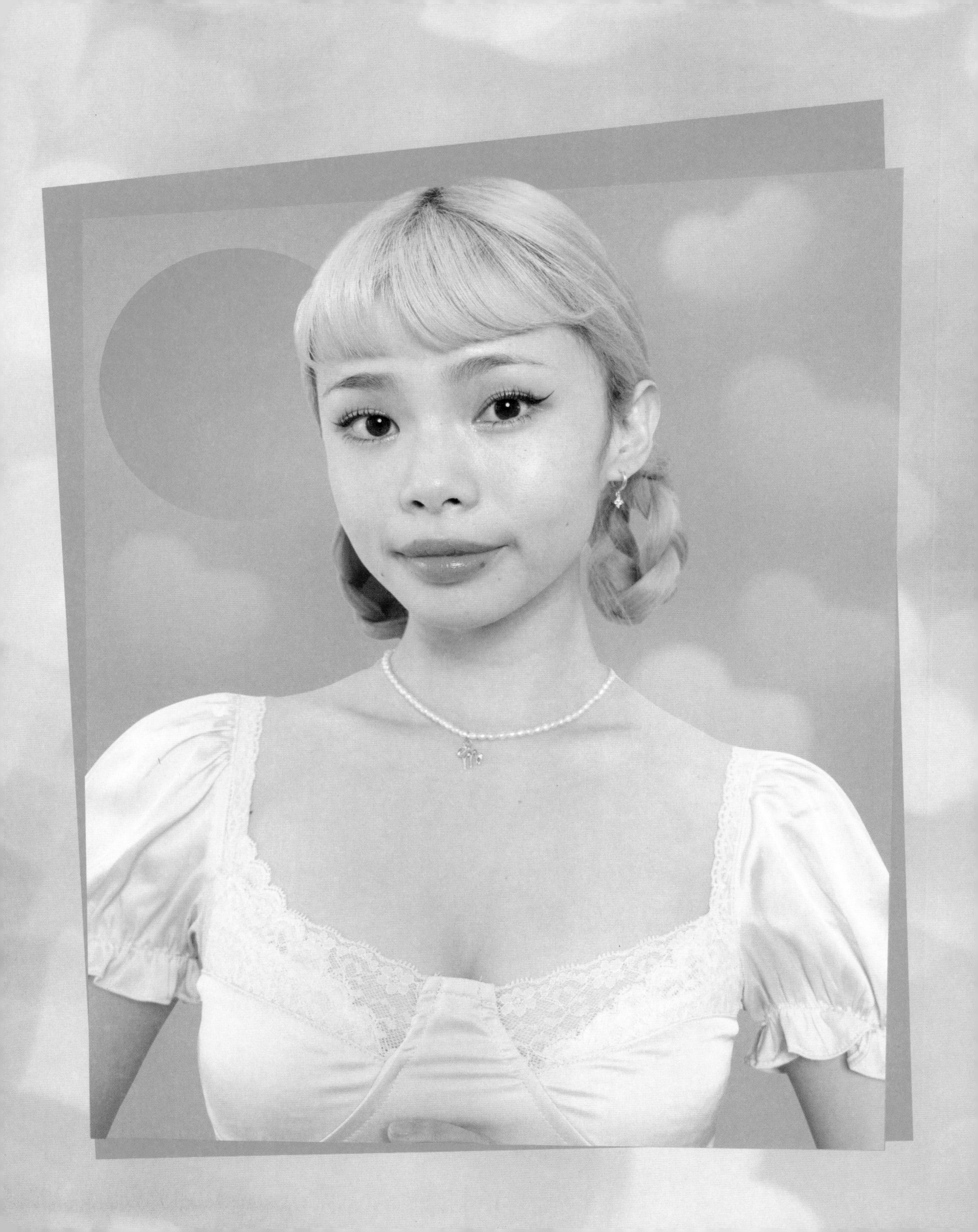

Nurse Joy

Pokémon

Double-looped pigtails are a popular anime hairstyle and are worn by many characters, including Kirari Momobami from *Kakegurui*. But when I thought about the first character I could remember seeing with this particular hairstyle, I immediately came up with Nurse Joy from my childhood days of hiding under the covers with my Nintendo DS playing *Pokémon*. This is personally one of my favorite cute hairstyles to wear on a daily basis. An added bonus: it's incredibly easy to create!

Tools

Rat-tail comb
• Elastics • Bobby pins •
1-inch straightening iron

1 Start with curled hair.

3 Braid each pigtail into a three-strand braid and secure with an elastic.

4 Loop each braid backward and wrap a few times around the base.

(a)

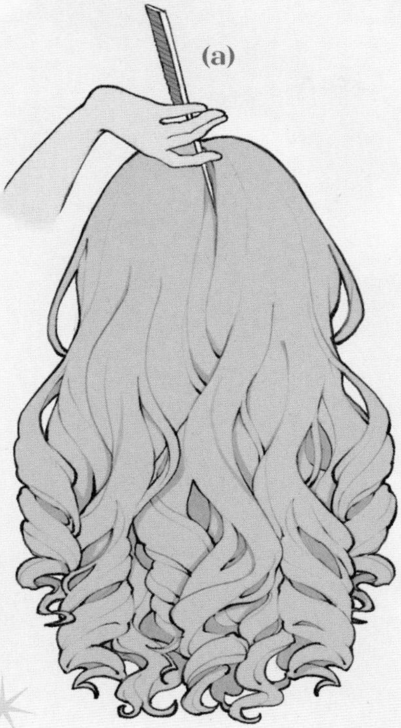

(b)

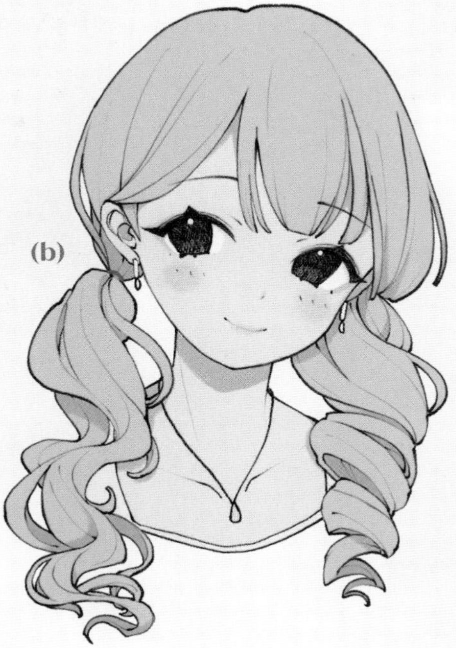

2 Using a rat-tail comb, section the hair straight down the middle (a) and gather into two low pigtails. Secure with elastics (b).

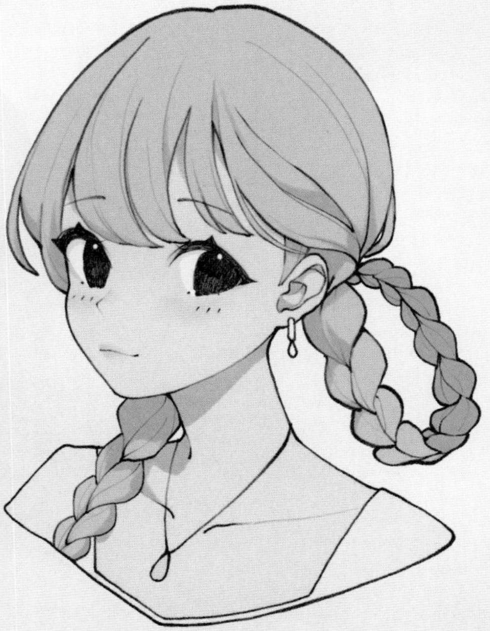

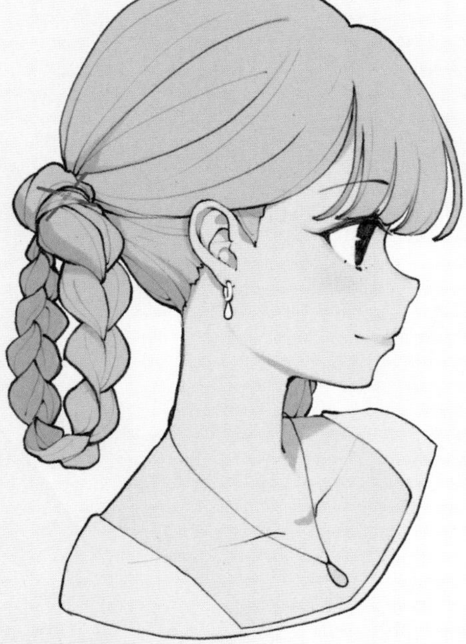

5 Secure with bobby pins.

6 Curl bangs inward with 1-inch straightening iron to complete the look.

Dawn

Pokémon

I love creating hairstyles based on two-dimensional characters because it allows me to think more creatively with hair. Based off photos alone, how do I shape and mold hair to replicate what I see on the screen? Dawn from *Pokémon Pearl* and *Diamond* is the perfect example of this process. With some unusual twists and turns, her hairstyle ends up being an incredibly cute and unique look!

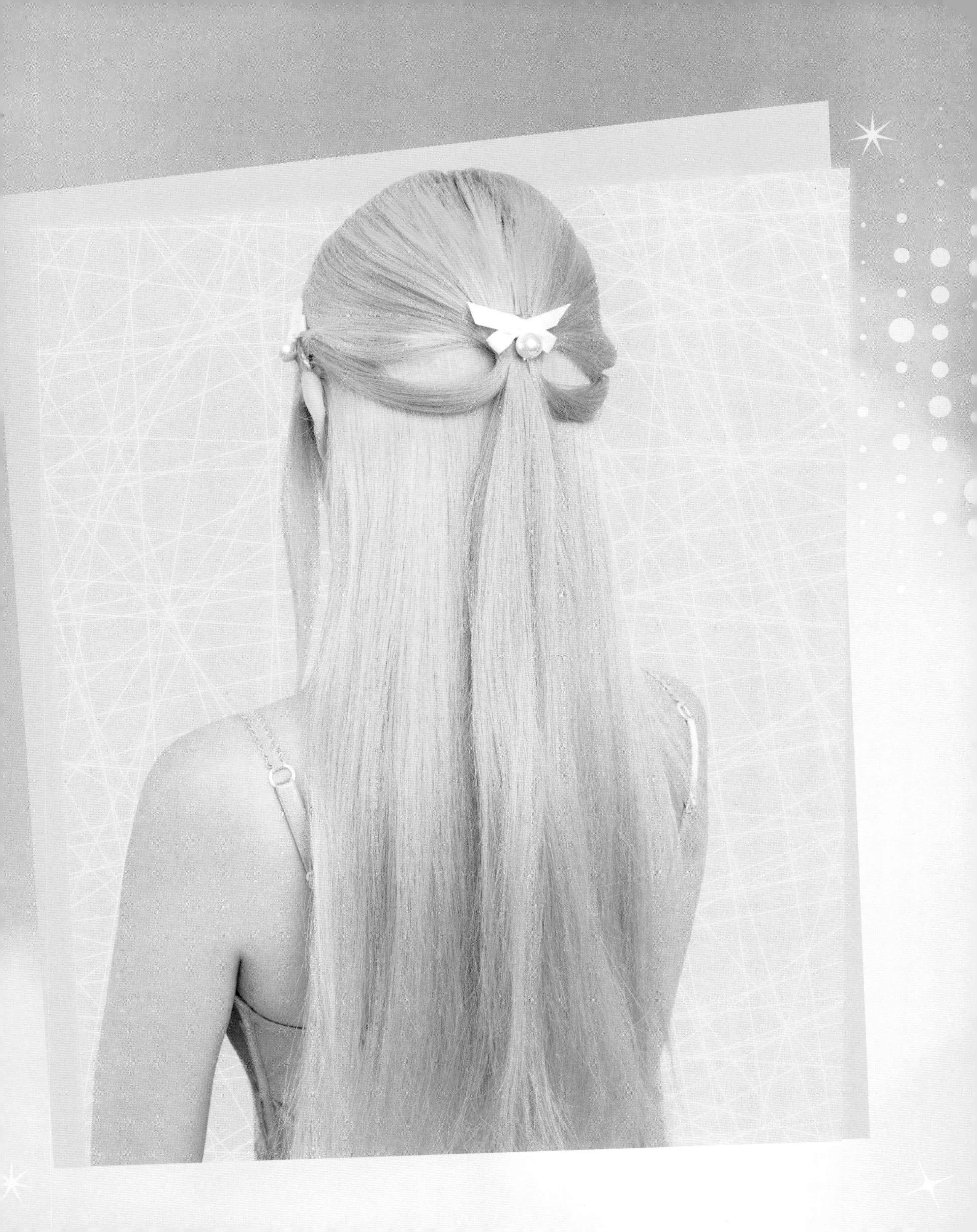

Tools

Elastics • Decorative hair clips • White hair ribbon • Pearl hair clip

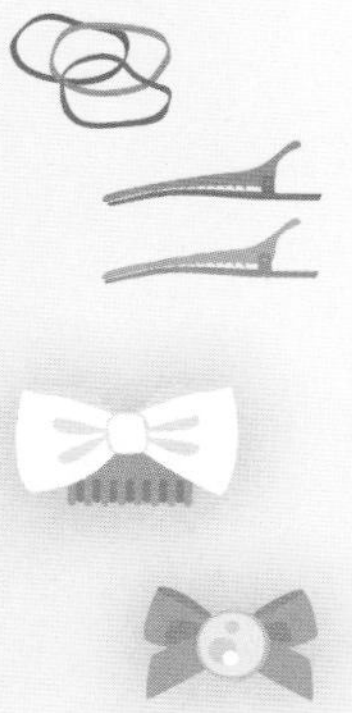

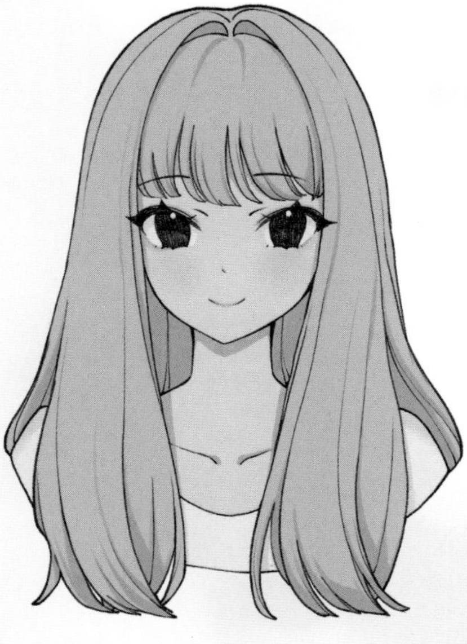

1 Start with straight hair.

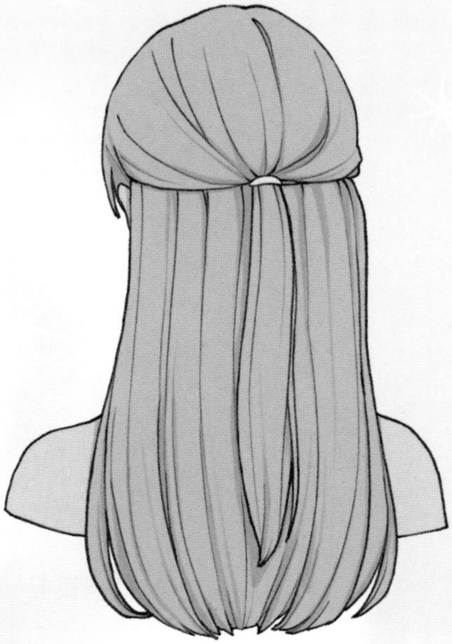

2 Gather the top half of hair into a mid-height half updo and tie with an elastic.

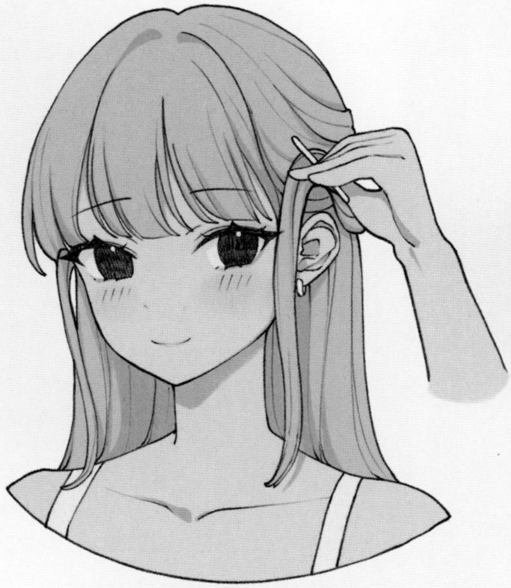

5 Hang the side sections over each ear and pin into place with decorative hair clips.

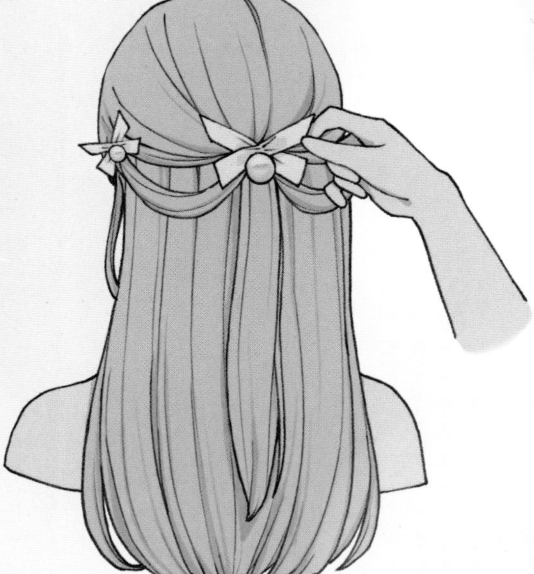

6 Use an accessory to hide the elastic in the back. (I've chosen a white ribbon and pearl hair clip to match the pair used above the ears.)

3 Holding the elastic as an anchor, gently loosen the top of the updo with your fingertips.

4 Split the ponytail of the updo into three sections.

Dawn wears this style in her competitions, but wears a hat in most other appearances, so your accessories are completely up to you! You can choose a hat for character accuracy or try something new to add your own personal touch.

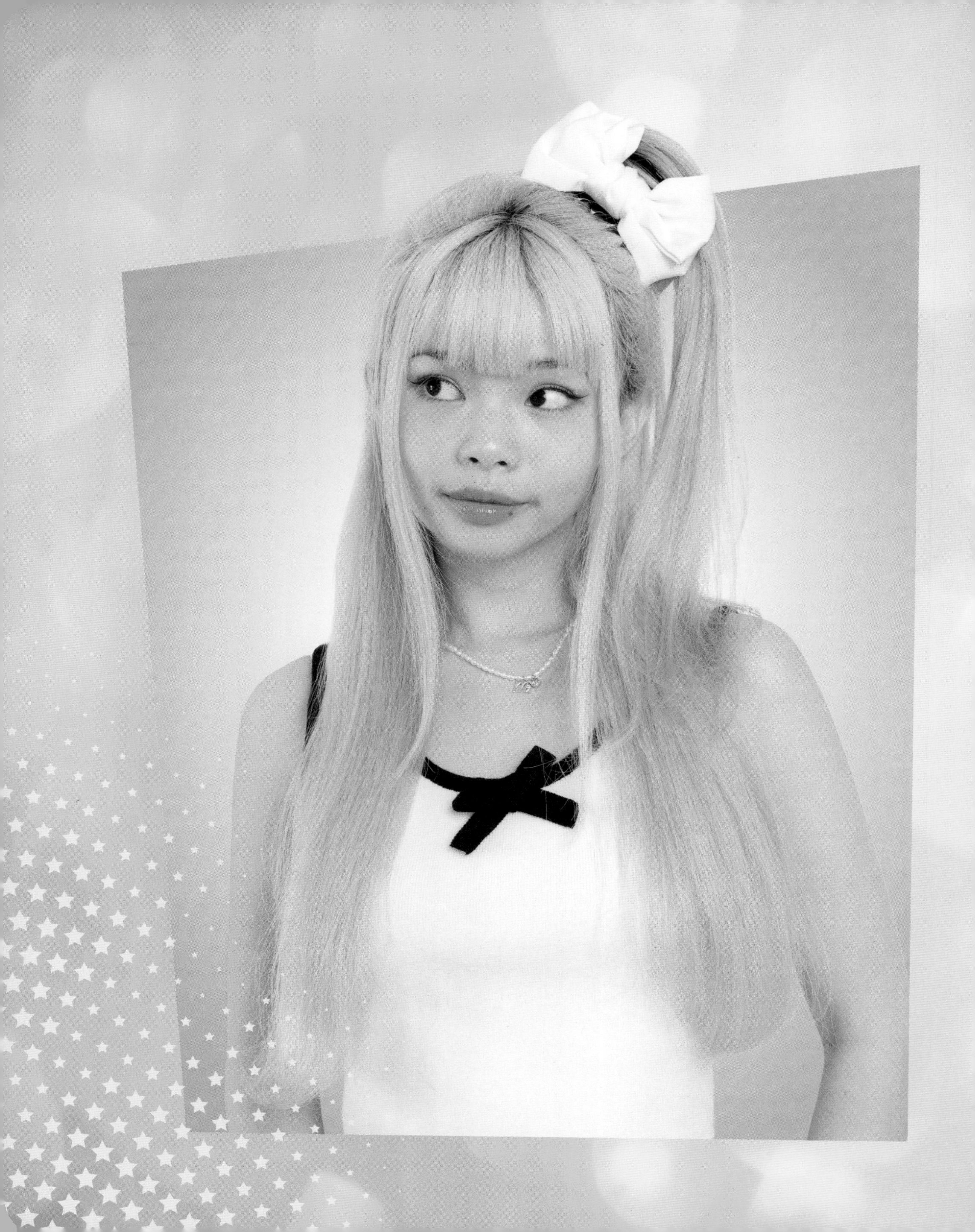

Hinamori Amu

Shugo Chara

If you're looking for hairstyles inspired by early 2000s fashion, I recommend looking toward anime from that era for inspiration. Hinamori from *Shugo Chara* wears a flipped-out style with a voluminous side ponytail that's reminiscent of popular hairstyles from that era. Here's how to easily achieve her look with one of my favorite hairstyle hacks! This easy tip helps achieve volume in any lazy-day hairstyle, and is something I personally wear the most in my daily life.

Tools

Rat-tail comb
- Hair spray • Elastics
- Boar-bristle brush
- Decorative hair claw
- Red hairclip (optional)

1 Start with straight hair with ends curled.

4 With a decorative hair claw, flip the ponytail upside down and clip at the base for more volume.

5 Flip the ponytail back around.

2 Using a rat-tail comb, section off 1-inch sections of hair to frame the face.

3 Gather the top section of hair into a left-sided half updo. Use hair spray and a boar-bristle brush to smooth the ponytail and secure with an elastic.

6 Optional: Instead of using a decorative hair claw, try using a plain hair claw with a red hair clip in the front for character accuracy.

Hoshina Utau

Shugo Chara

Using my hair claw hack (see the Hinamori Amu style, page 53), you can transform dull ponytails and pigtails into voluminous looks without using hair extensions. Hoshina Utau from *Shugo Chara* is a perfect example to share how to create the ultimate voluminous twin tails that are iconic in anime.

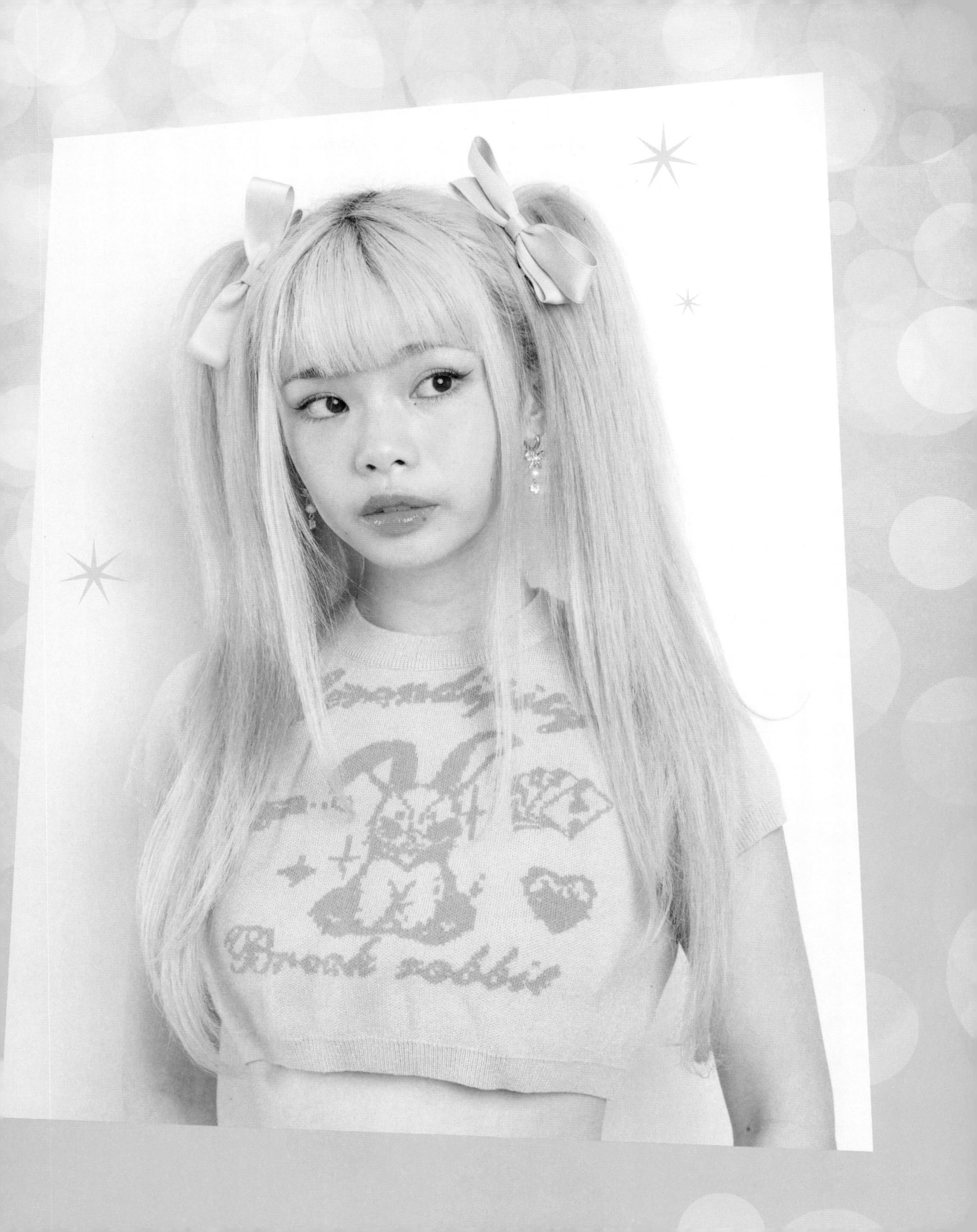

Tools

Rat-tail comb • Elastics • Hair spray • Boar-bristle brush • Two small hair claws • Ribbons for accessorizing

1 Start with straight hair.

4 Split each pigtail in half. Flip upward and clip at the base with a small hair claw to create volume.

2 Using a rat-tail comb, section off 1-inch sections of hair to frame the face.

3 Gather the rest of the hair into two high pigtails and secure with elastics. Use hair spray at the roots and a boar-bristle brush to smooth out flyaways for tidy-looking pigtails.

5 Accessorize with two ribbons to hide the elastics.

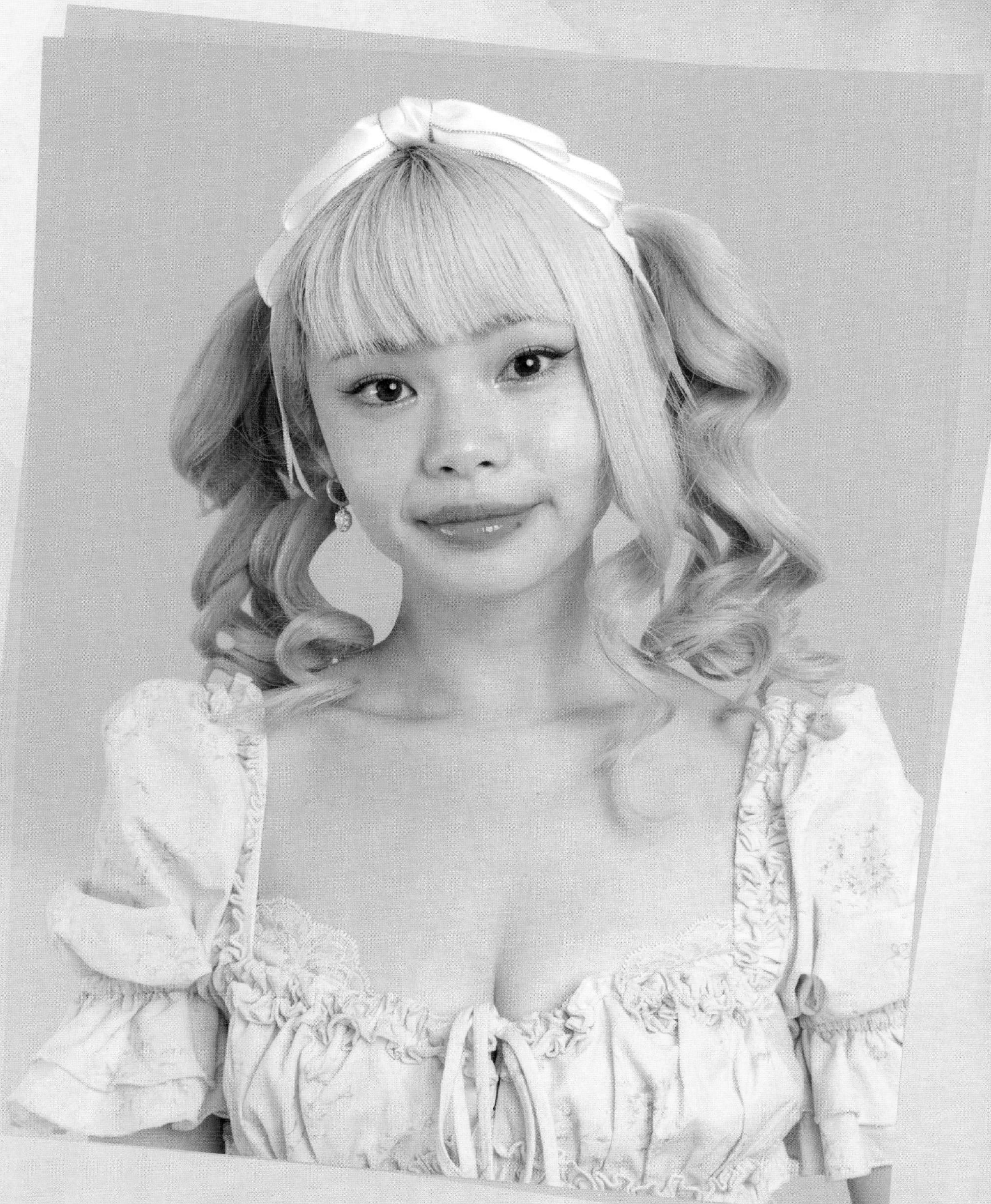

Elizabeth Midford

Kuroshitsuji

Elizabeth Midford, also known as Lizzy, from *Kuroshitsuji* wears one of my personal favorite anime hairstyles of all time. These large curls go by several different names but are most commonly known as drill curls. Drill curls have been an iconic look in anime for decades, as you can see them worn by Mami Tomoe from *Madoka Magica*, Biscuit Krueger from *Hunter x Hunter*, and many more.

Because this hairstyle exposes the hair to quite a lot of heat, be sure to always start with a heat protection product before styling, to keep your hair healthy. The use of heat protection also helps curls stay soft and bouncy after styling!

Tools

Heat protection product • Rat-tail comb • Elastics • 1-inch-barrel curling wand • Hair clips • Headband

1 Start with straight hair, prepped and primed with heat protection product.

2 Using a rat-tail comb, section off a 2-inch section of hair on the left side.

(a)

(b)

5 Gently pin each curl with a clip (a) and allow to completely cool before releasing for perfect ringlets (b).

3 Gather the remaining hair into two high pigtails and secure with elastics.

4 With a 1-inch curling wand, curl 1-inch sections of hair at a time.

6 Accessorize with a headband.

Lacus Clyne

Gundam Seed Destiny ✦ Updo Version

I may be biased, but pink-haired anime girls are the ultimate hair inspirations! Lacus Clyne wears a few different hairstyles with her long pink hair throughout *Gundam Seed Destiny*, but this style is one of my favorites of her looks. She usually wears her hair straight down, but this braided bun is a great way to add technique, texture, and volume to an otherwise plain half updo.

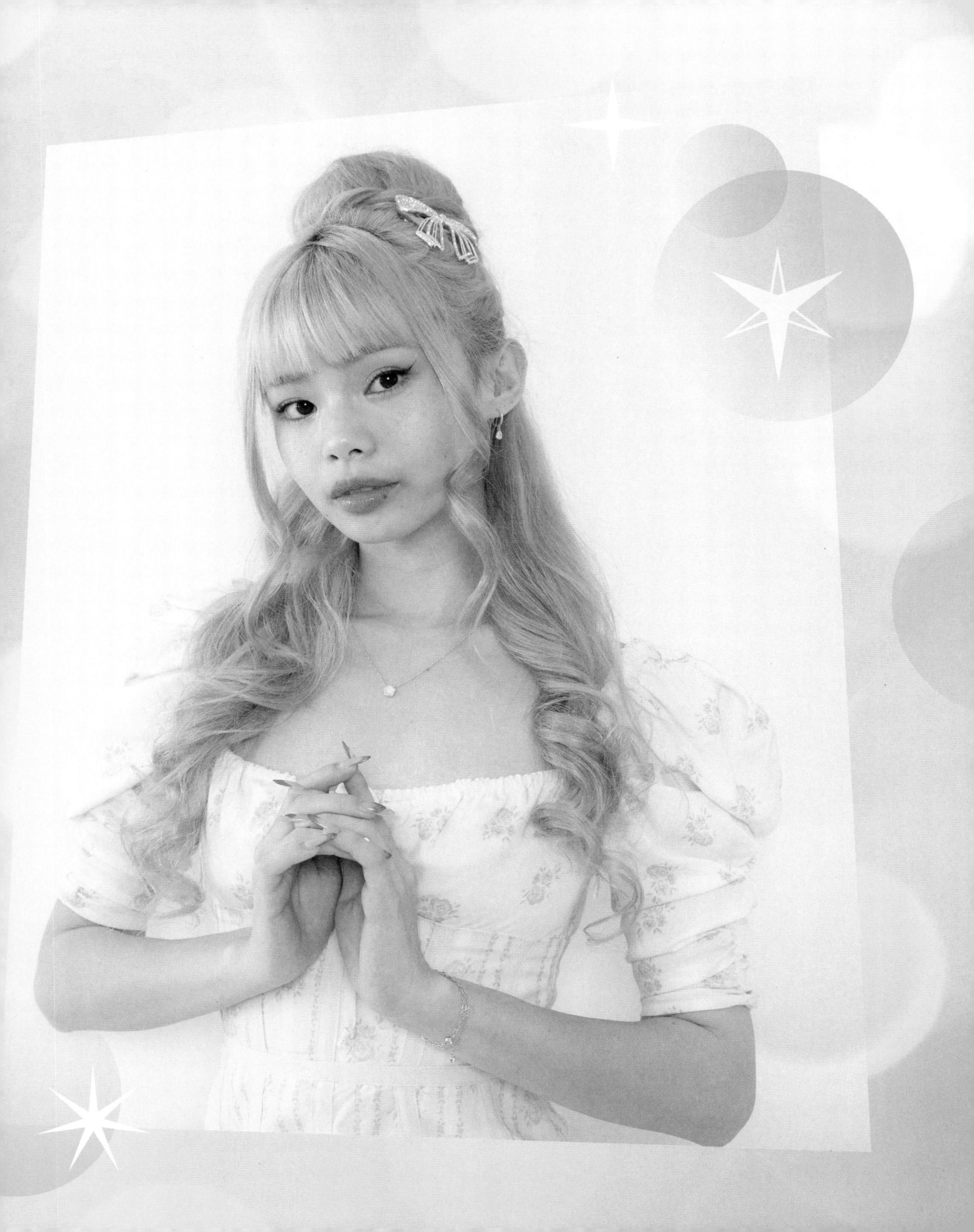

Tools

Rat-tail comb • Bun maker • Bobby pins • Elastics • Yellow hair clip (optional)

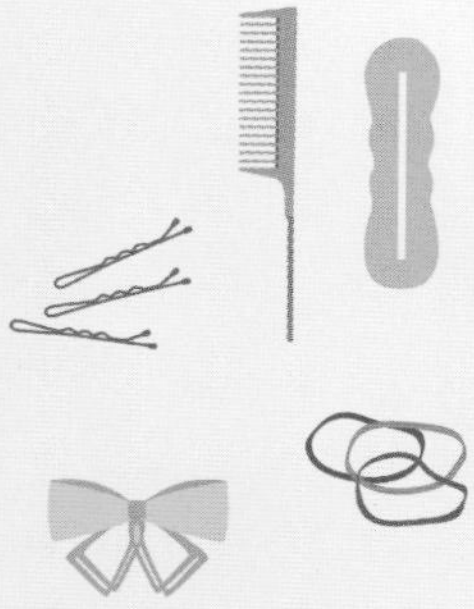

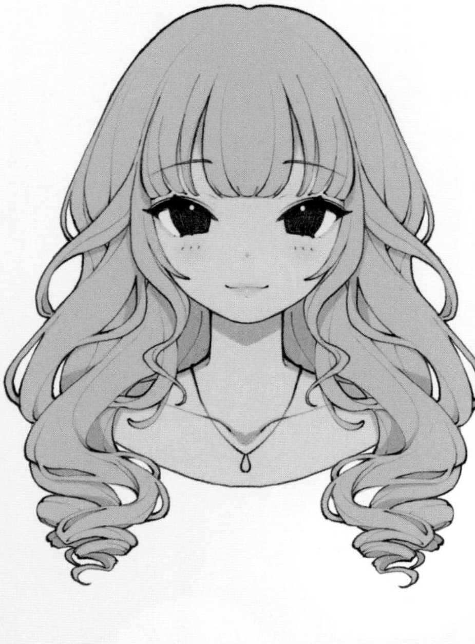

1 Start with curled hair.

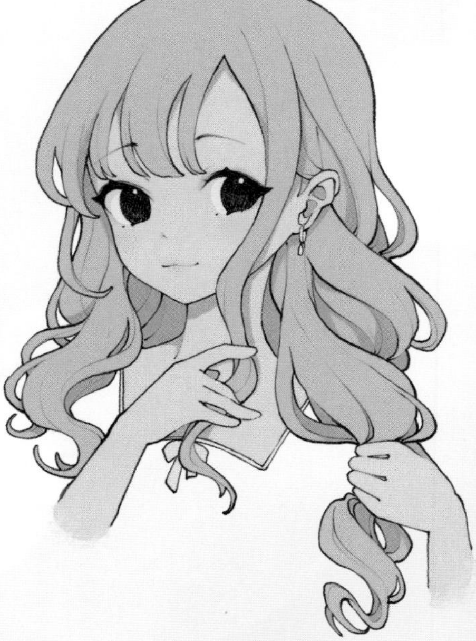

2 Using a rat-tail comb, section off 1-inch sections of hair to frame the face.

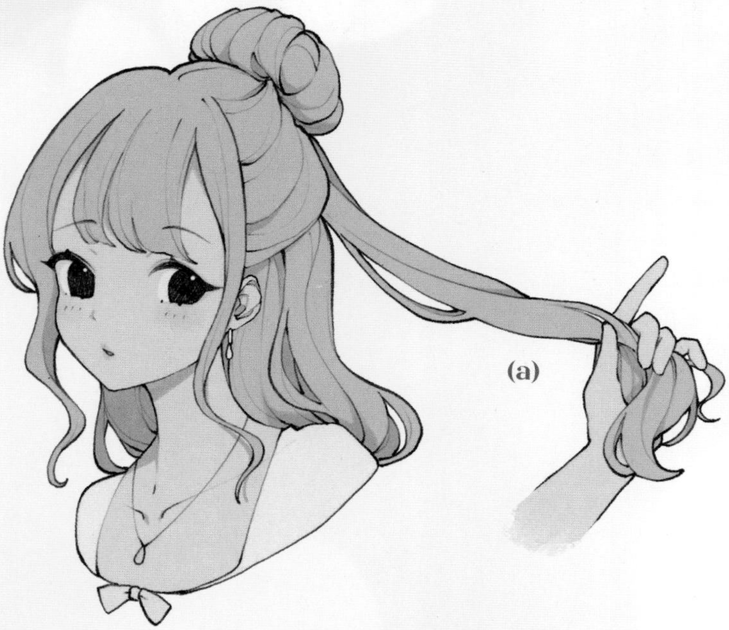
(a)

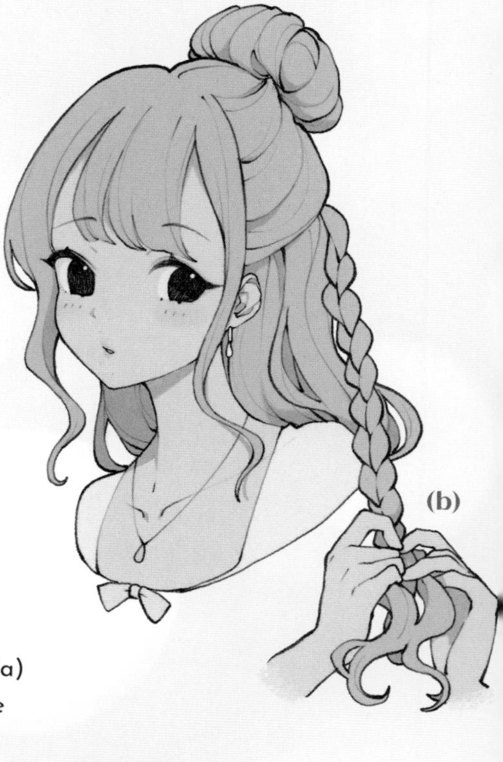
(b)

5 Braid the remaining 2 inches of hair (a) into a loose three-strand braid. Secure with an elastic (b).

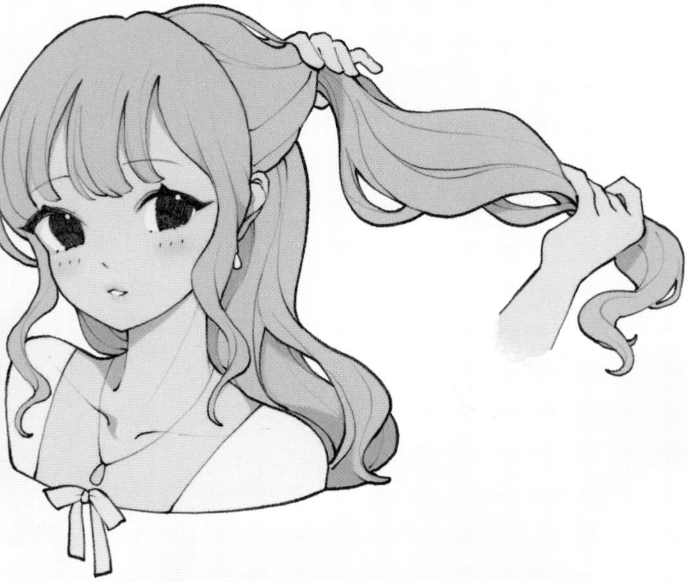

3 Gather the top section of hair to create a half updo. Secure with an elastic.

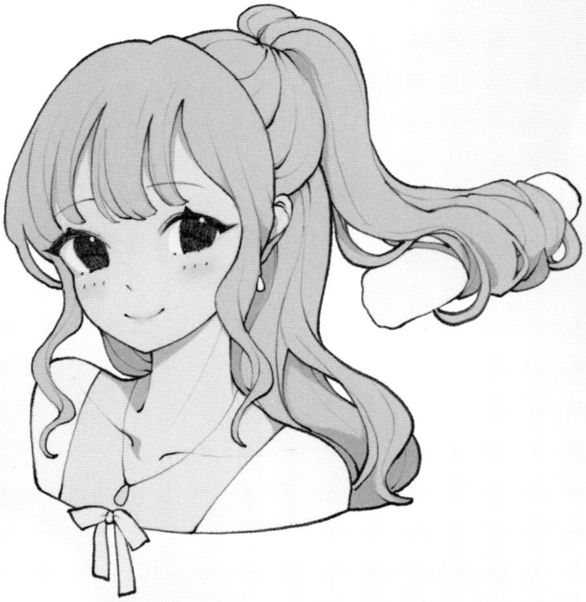

4 Leaving a 2-inch section of hair, gather the rest of the updo ponytail and create a loose fluffy bun with a bun maker and pin into place.

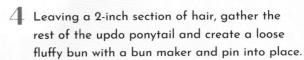

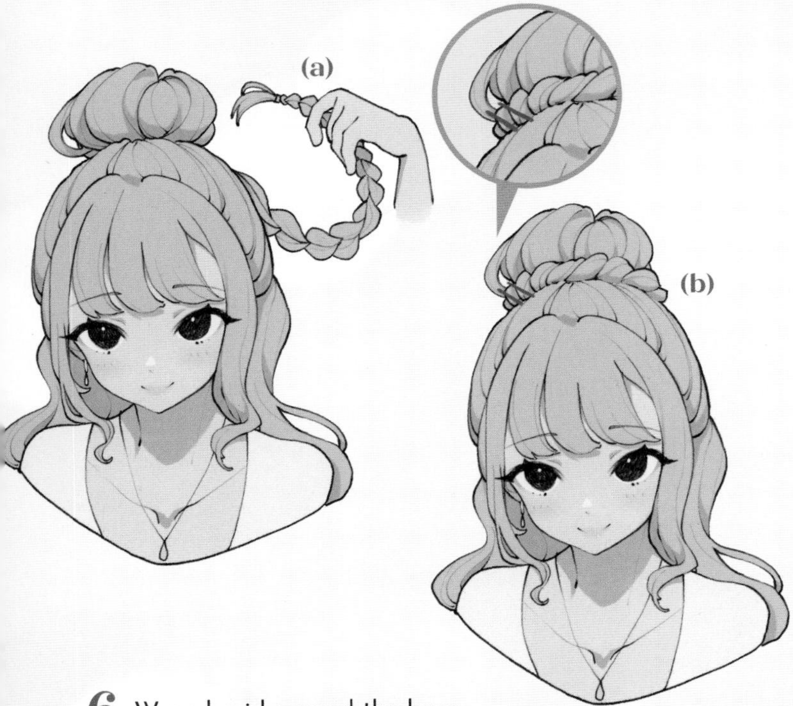
(a)
(b)

6 Wrap braid around the base of the bun (a) and pin into place (b).

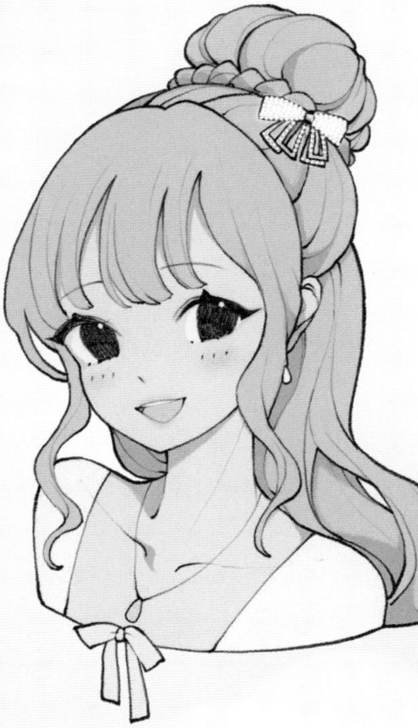

7 Accessorize with a yellow hair clip, if desired.

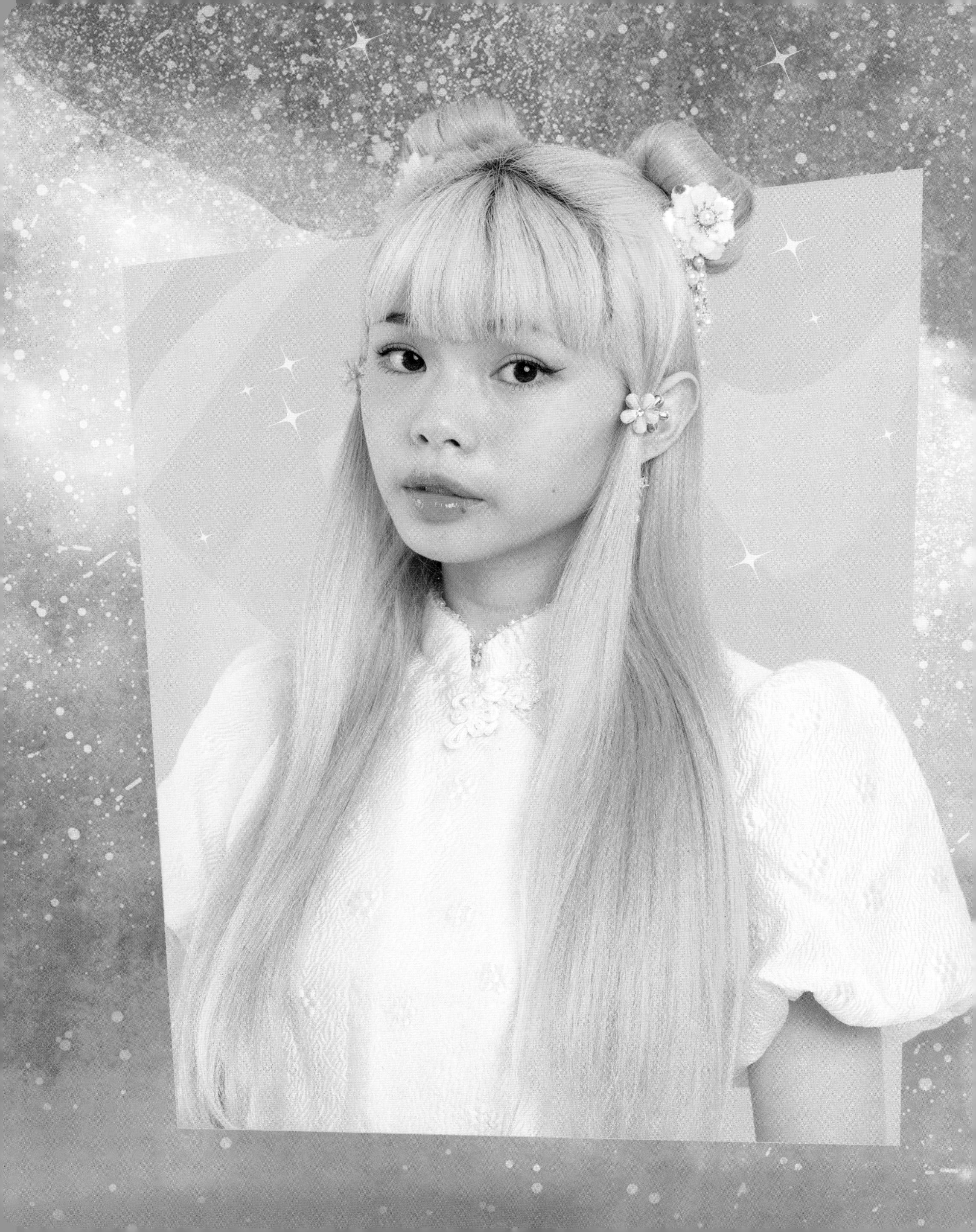

Shampoo

Ranma ½

Hairstyles on Chinese characters in anime are among some of my personal favorite looks to recreate, as they often incorporate cute buns and accessories. Think Ran-Mao from *Kuroshitsuji*, Meiling Li from *Cardcaptor Sakura*, and most famously, Chun-Li from *Street Fighter*. Shampoo from *Ranma ½* wears two perfectly round buns with two little pigtails framing her face.

Tools

Rat-tail comb • Two bun makers •Bobby pins • Elastics • Decorative hair clips

1 Start with straight hair with the ends curled inward.

2 Using a rat-tail comb, section off 2-inch sections of hair above the ear to frame the face, then leave alone for now.

4 Gather the 2-inch sections of hair in the front and secure them at the temple with an elastic.

5 Gently loosen with fingertips to create volume.

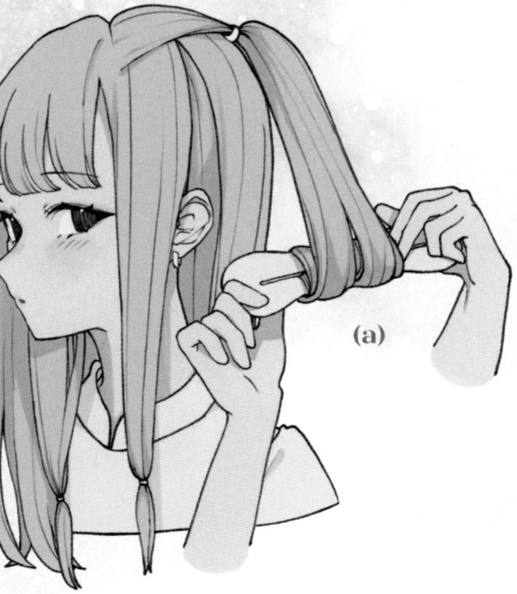
(a)

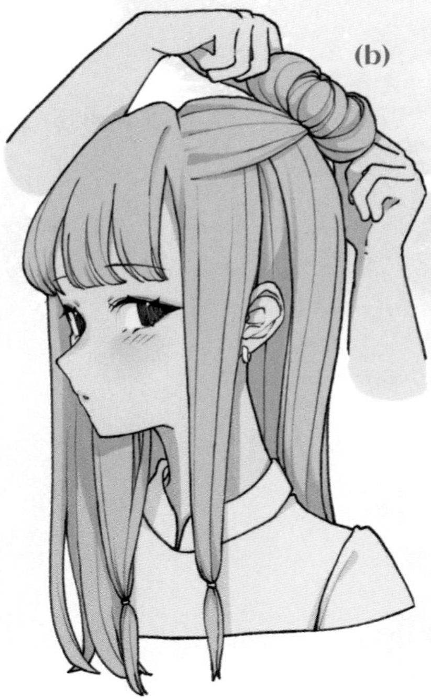
(b)

3 Create two half updo pigtails, one on either side of the head, then use small bun makers to create fluffy buns (a) and pin into place (b).

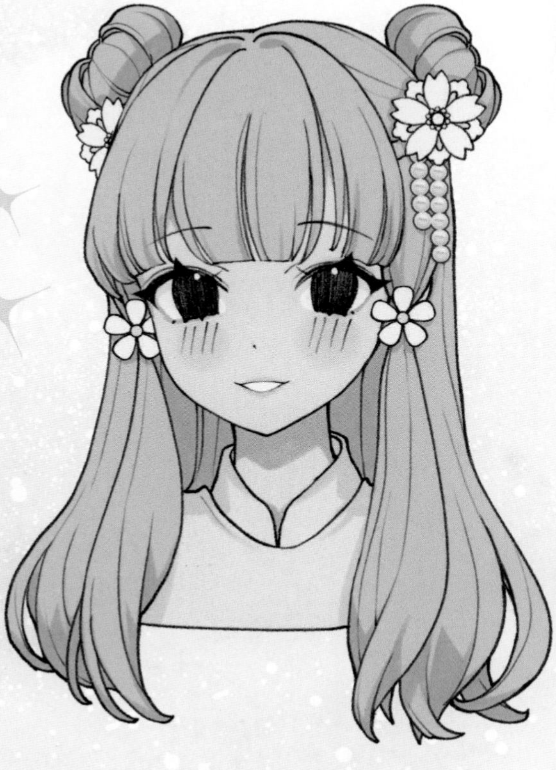

6 Accessorize at the base of the bun and at the temples with decorative clips to hide the elastics. Shampoo wears her front-framing pieces with hair ties tied near the bottom, but I find that my version is a much easier alternative to wear, as it keeps the hair in place longer throughout the day.

Marie Antoinette

The Rose of Versailles

The Rose of Versailles is arguably one of the most iconic vintage anime series, making appearances even on high-fashion runways for luxury brands like Moschino. This is the oldest series that we'll be covering in this book, with its debut in the 1970s. Based off the real-life historical figure, the character Marie Antoinette wears period-accurate regal ringlet curls with an anime-inspired twist. These spiral curls will definitely bring an air of aristocracy to your look.

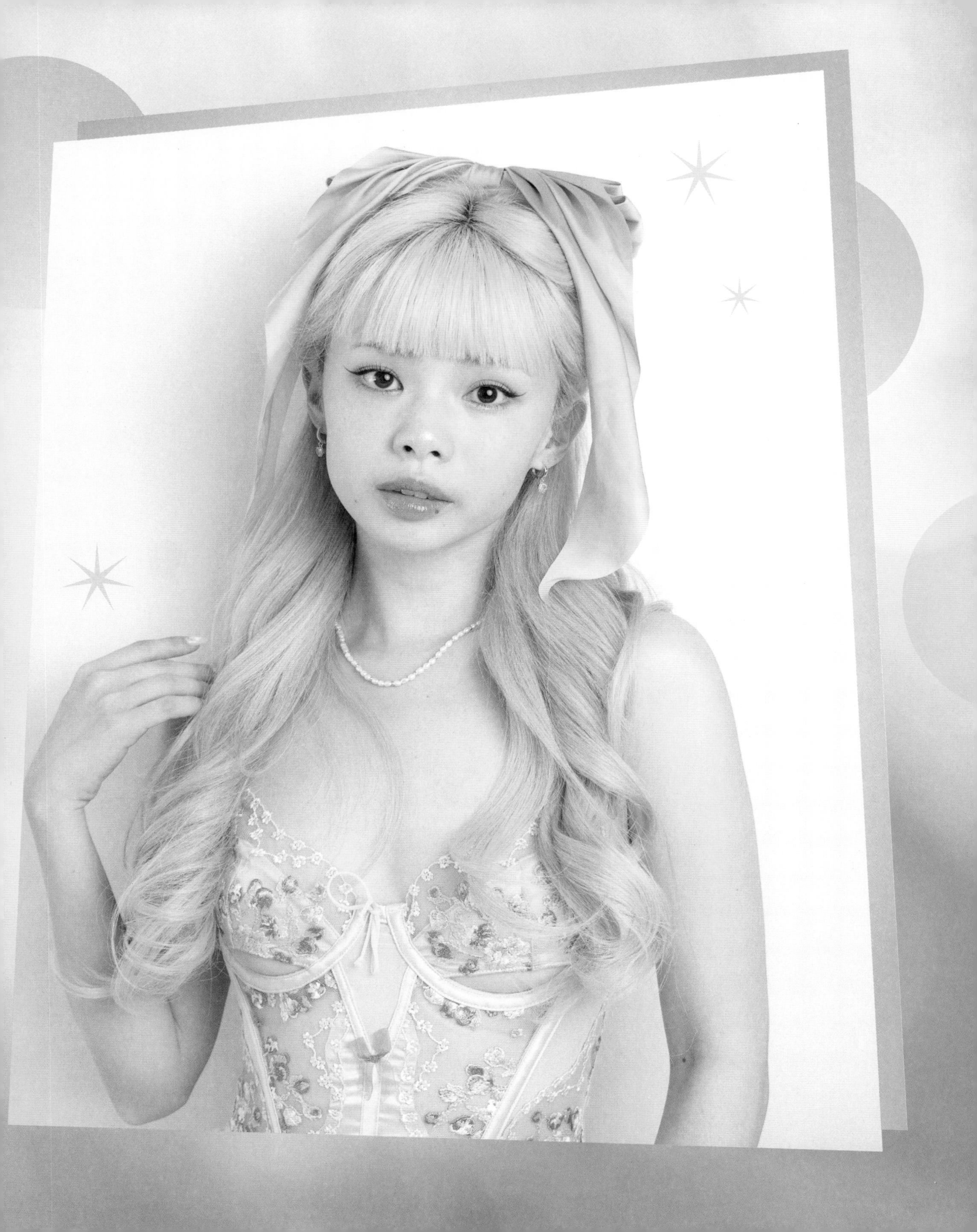

Tools

Detangling hairbrush • Elastics • 1½-inch-barrel curling iron • Oversized bow hair clip

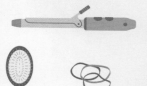

1 Start with straight hair.

4 With a 1½-inch-barrel curling iron, loosely curl each section of hair into loose spirals.

5 Tighten the base of the high ponytail and maneuver the hair to frame the face.

2 Begin by gathering the top third of the hair into a high ponytail.

3 Use a hairbrush to gently smooth out flyaways and secure with an elastic.

6 With an oversized bow hair clip, pin in the center of the elastic to keep the hair in place.

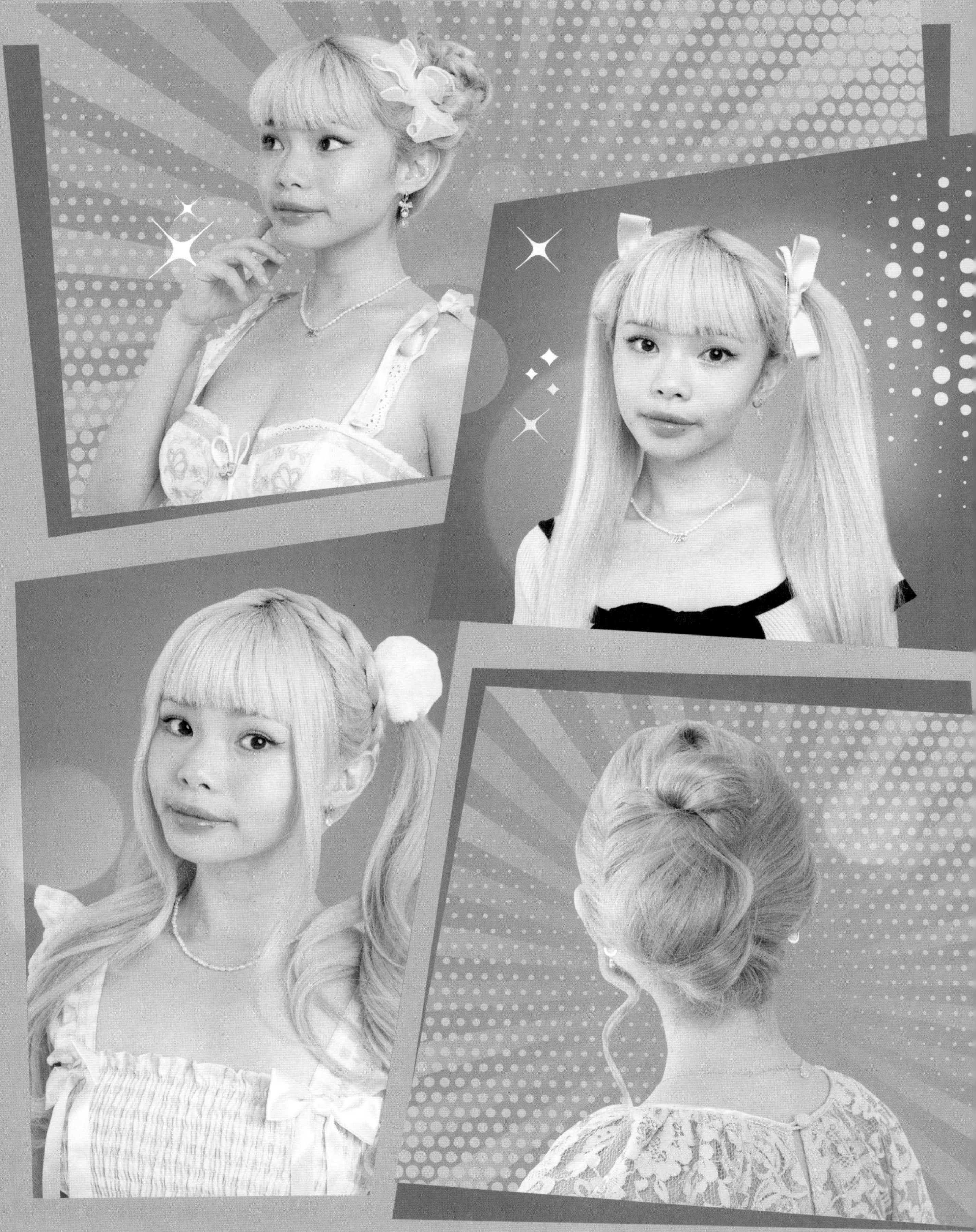

INTERMEDIATE

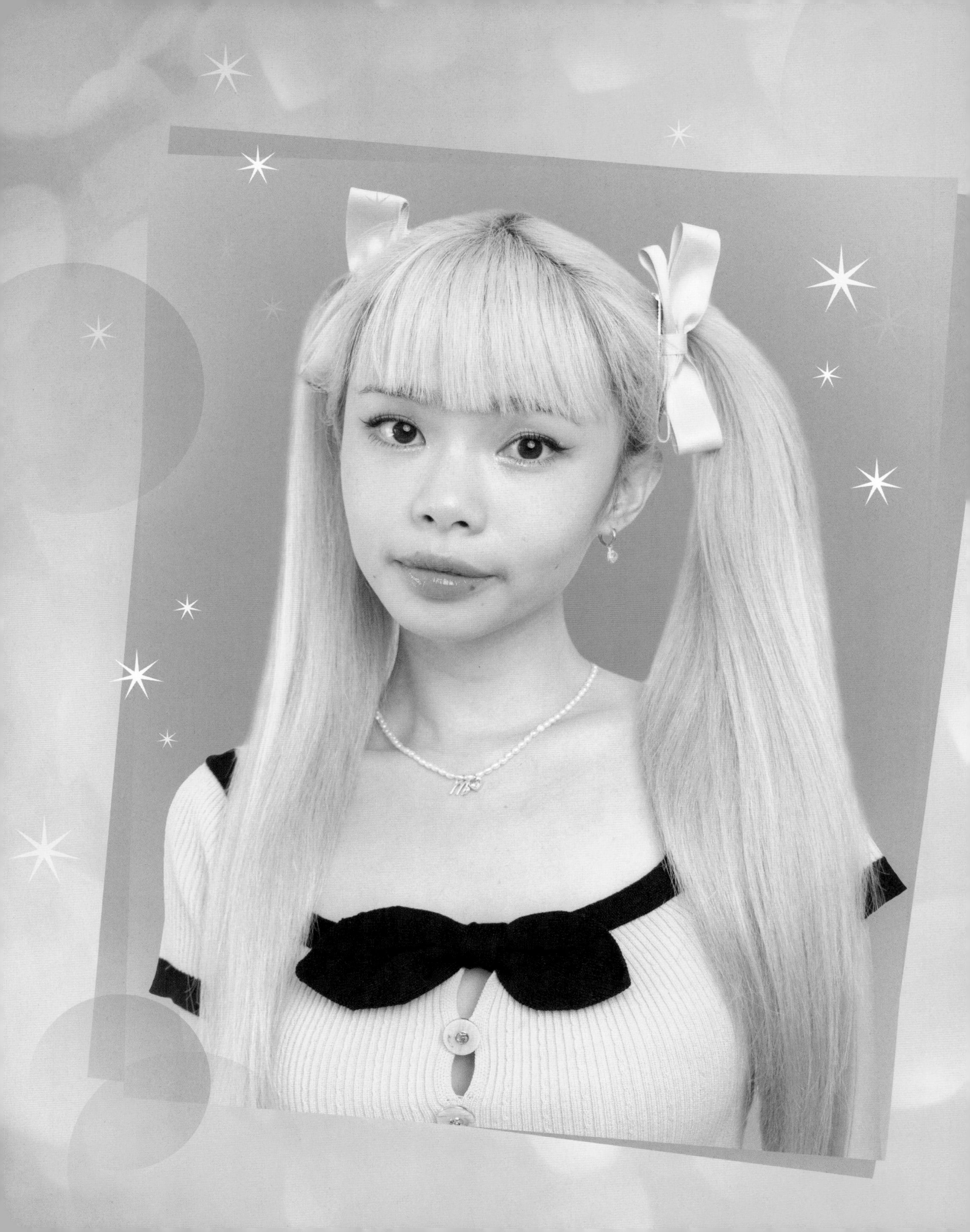

Sakurada Miwako

Paradise Kiss ✦ Voluminous Twin Tails

When it comes to iconic pink-haired anime characters, Sakurada Miwako from *Paradise Kiss*, written by Ai Yazawa, is one of the first characters that comes to mind. Yazawa's shoujo manga, a genre for girls and young women, is a treasure trove of inspiration for hair and fashion styles. Miwako, in particular, wears many different hairstyles throughout the series, some of which I'll be covering in this book.

Anime twin tails are always perfectly bouncy, voluminous, and larger than life. Ever wondered how to create them in the real world? With my easy technique and the help of hair extensions, anyone can create this iconic anime hairstyle.

Tools

Rat-tail comb • Elastics • Hair extensions • Hair spray • Boar-bristle brush • Two large hair bows

1 Start with straight hair.

2 Using a rat-tail comb, part the hair 2 inches from the middle part.

6 Flip a two-weft extension upside down and clip onto the bottom of the pigtail.

7 Flip the pigtail of your hair over the bottom extension.

3 Using a rat-tail comb, take a 2-inch section of hair on the side of the head.

4 Gather into a pigtail and secure with an elastic. Repeat on the other side.

5 Flip the pigtail over your head.

8 Clip a second two-weft extension over the top of the pigtail, creating a sandwich of long extensions surrounding the small pigtail. Repeat on the other pigtail.

9 Gather the rest of the hair into two high pigtails around the extensions. Brush smooth with hair spray and a boar-bristle brush and tie with two elastics.

10 Accessorize with two hair bows to hide the elastics.

Sakurada Miwako

Paradise Kiss ◆ Curly Pigtails

I may be a little biased because I love her so much, but Miwako's curly pigtails are perhaps one of the most iconic and stylish pink anime hairstyles. This look takes a bit of DIY and overnight preparation, so be prepared to get a little crafty.

With this hairstyle, Miwako wears a variation of ringlet curls. They were originally popularized in ancient society among the aristocracy, dating back to ancient Roman times. These unique curls were painstakingly created by wrapping hair tightly around hot rods, but the method we'll be using is a hair-friendly, heat-free method. All you need are a couple pieces of scrap fabric to create these gorgeous (and versatile) rag curls.

Tools

15 to 20 pieces of scrap fabric, 2 inches wide and 8 inches long • Elastics • Hair spray • White pom-pom hair ties • Hair oil and/or hair wax (optional) • Hair dryer (optional)

1 Begin with lightly damp hair, only about 70 percent dry.

2 Take a 1-inch section of hair and wrap it around the fabric.

6 Gently untie each bundle to release the curls. Only use fingers to gently comb through.

7 Tie into two high pigtails and secure with elastics. Spray with hair spray to keep everything in place. Repeat on the other pigtail.

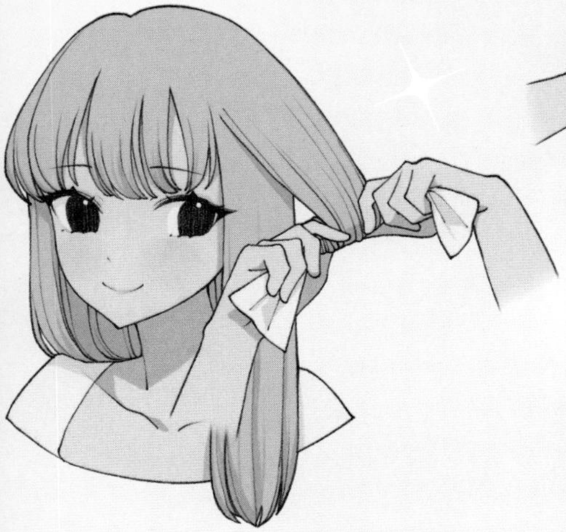

3 Begin by wrapping the end of the hair around the fabric to secure it in place, then roll upward to the top of the head.

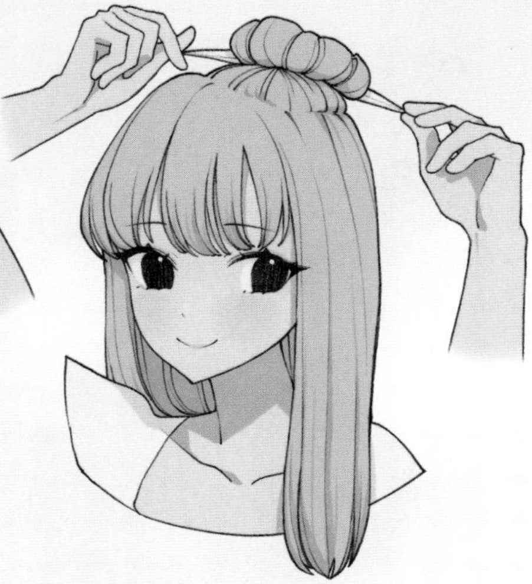

4 Tie the two ends of the fabric piece together to create a little bundle of hair. Repeat the process until all the hair is curled.

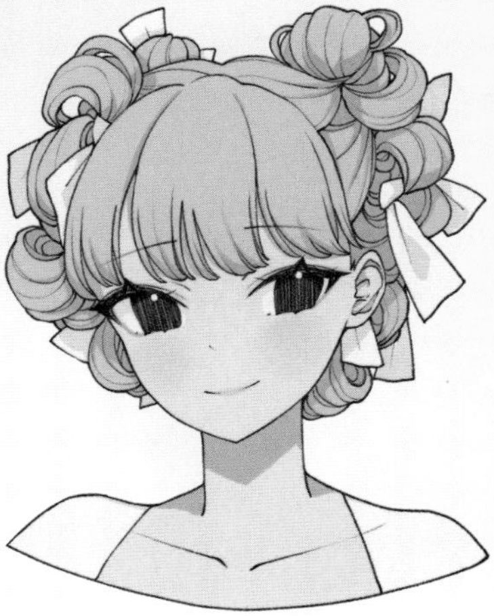

5 Allow the hair to fully dry either overnight for the heatless method, or with a hair dryer for quicker results.

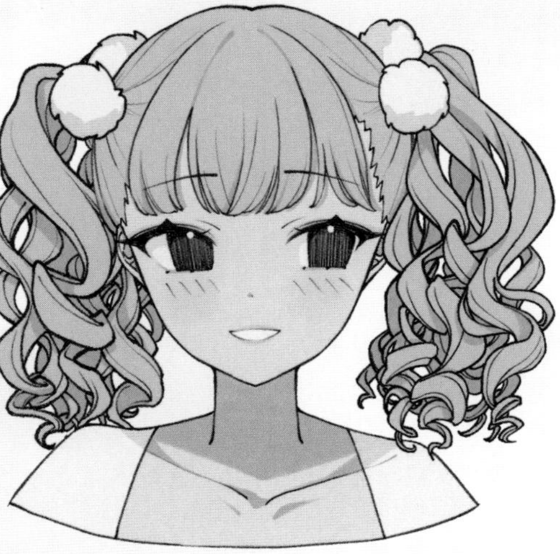

8 Accessorize with white fluffy pom-pom hair ties to finish the look.

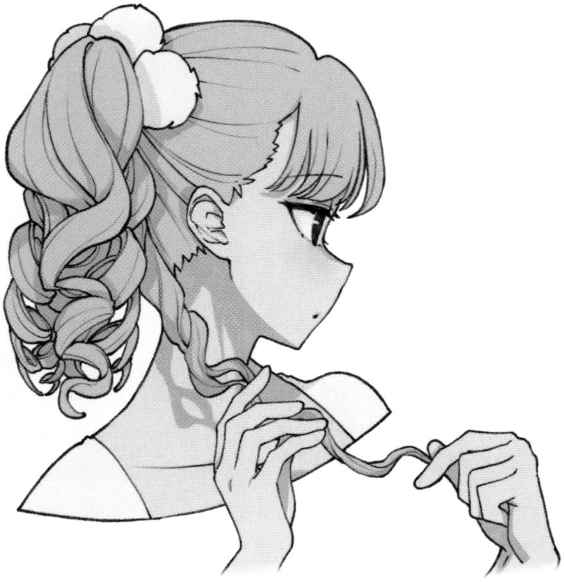

9 Optional: Gently apply hair oil and/or hair wax to smooth and define the curls.

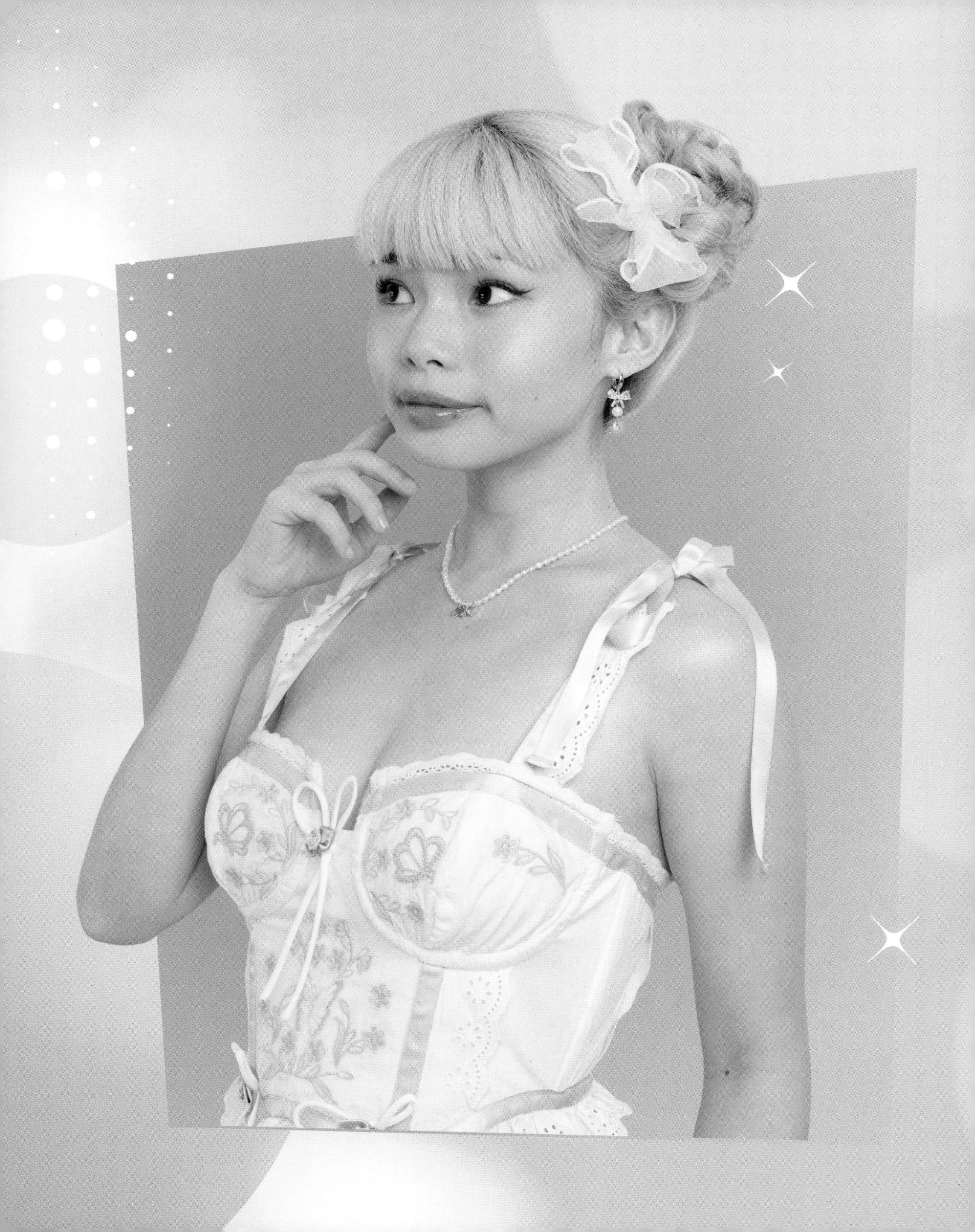

Sakurada Miwako

Paradise Kiss ◆ Curly Buns

Now that you know how to create perfect ringlet curls using the rag curl method as shown in the tutorial for Miwako's curly pigtails (page 83), it's time to utilize that technique for another one of Miwako's signature hairstyles. As you learn more techniques throughout this book, you'll find it easier to layer different techniques to create increasingly complex hairstyles. By the end of this book, the knowledge gained will have you easily recreating any anime hairstyle, or even inventing some of your own!

Tools

15 to 20 pieces of scrap fabric, 2 inches wide and 8 inches long • Elastics • Bobby pins • Hair spray

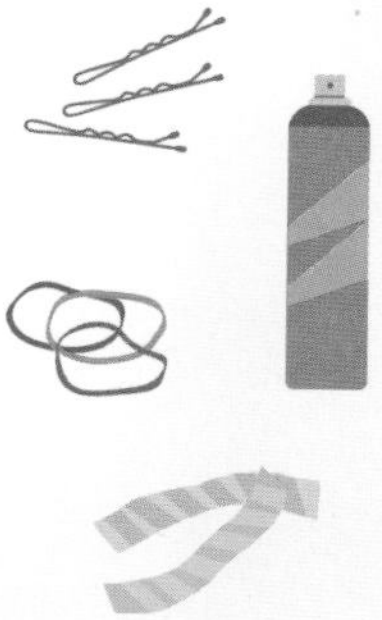

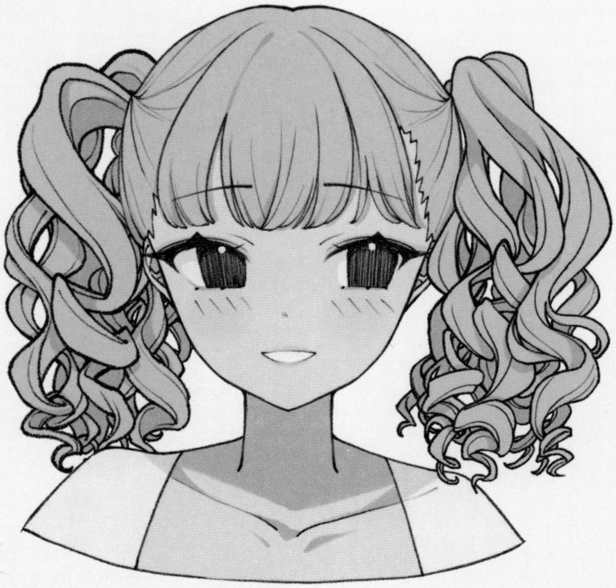

1 Prepare hair with rag curls, as seen in the instructions for Miwako's curly pigtails (see page 83). Once curled, tie hair into two high pigtails and secure with elastics.

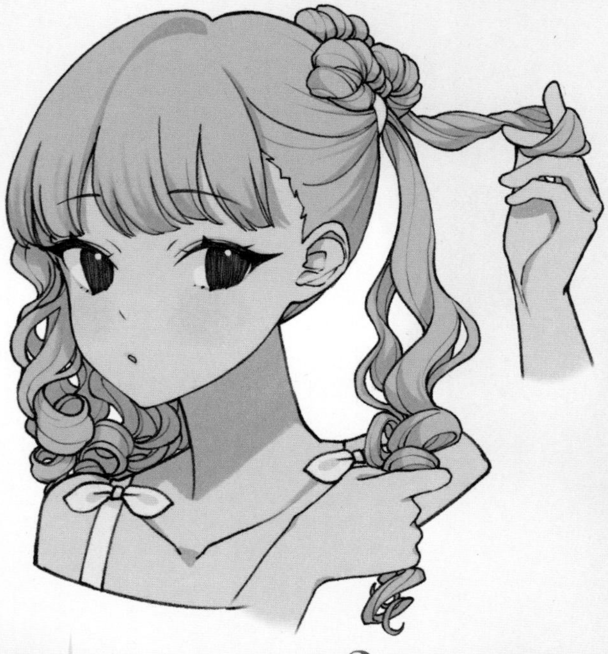

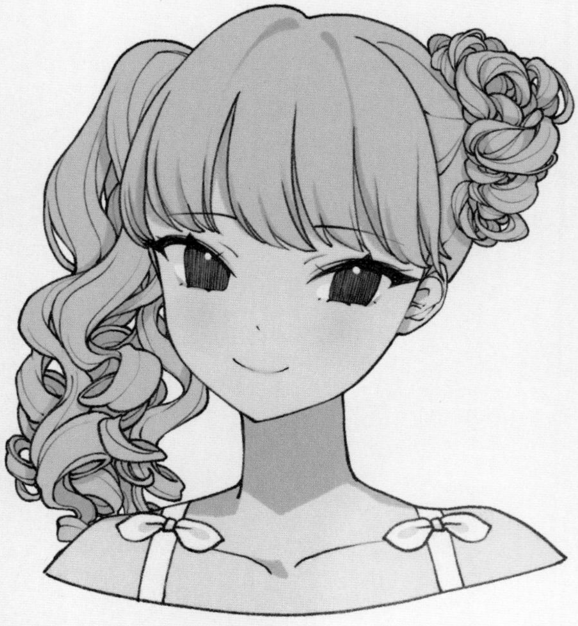

3 Repeat until all curls are rolled into a fluffy bun.

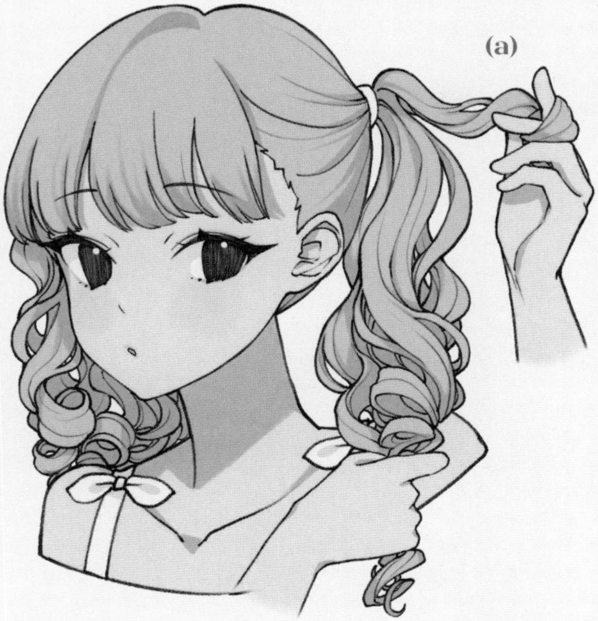
(a)

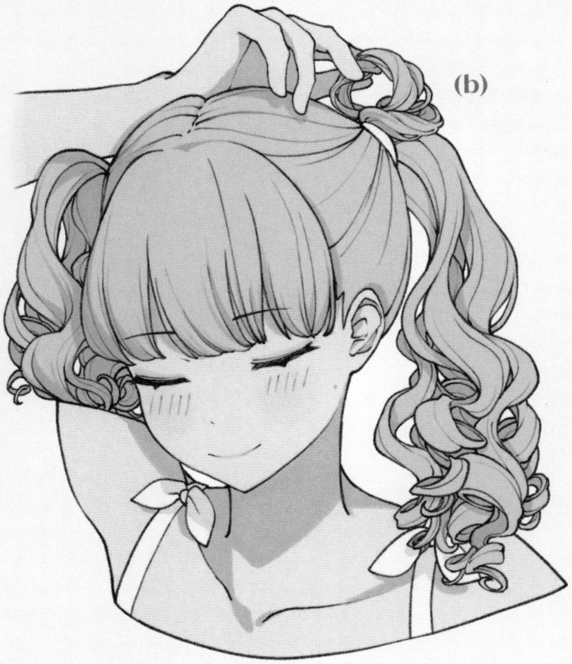
(b)

2 Twist 1-inch sections of curls around two fingers (a) and roll them up toward the head; pin the curls in place (b).

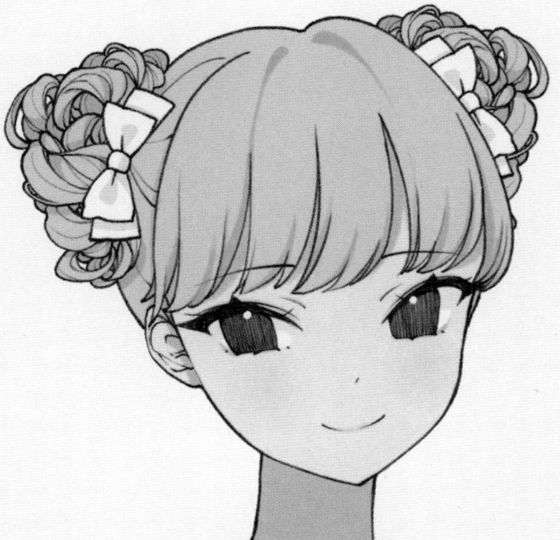

4 Spray with hair spray to keep in place. This completes Miwako's look, but accessorize as you like!

Yor Forger

Spy x Family ◆ Daily Updo Version

Spy x Family is a widely popular series that has experienced global success reaching far beyond Japan, and it's also one of my personal favorites! Yor Forger wears one of the most interesting hairstyles I've seen to date, and there are many ways to recreate her look. This is one of my favorite ways to easily achieve her updo, and you can even recreate it on short hair. I speak from experience, as this braided updo is something I used to wear on a daily basis when I had chin-length hair!

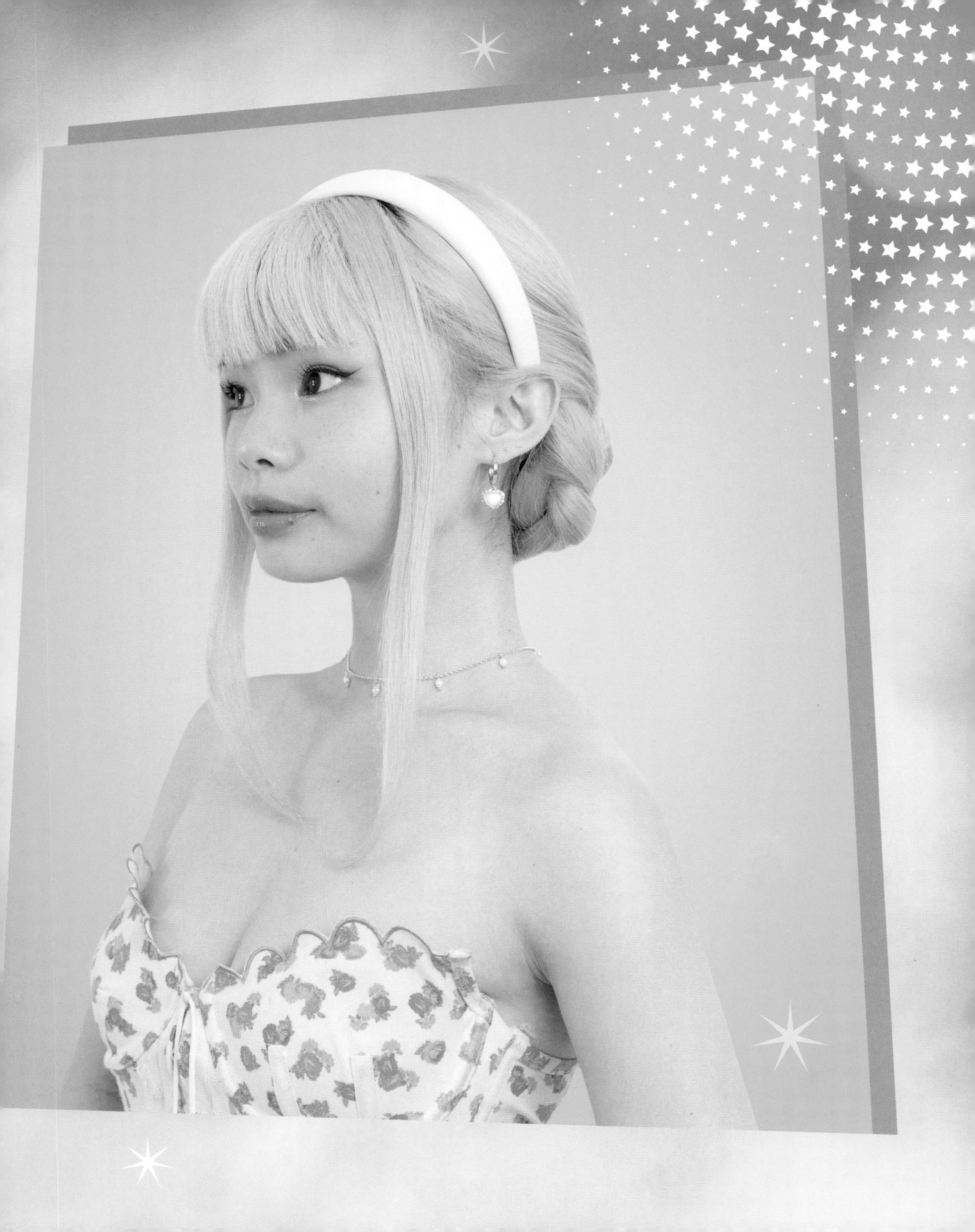

Tools

Rat-tail comb
- Elastics • Bobby pins
- White headband

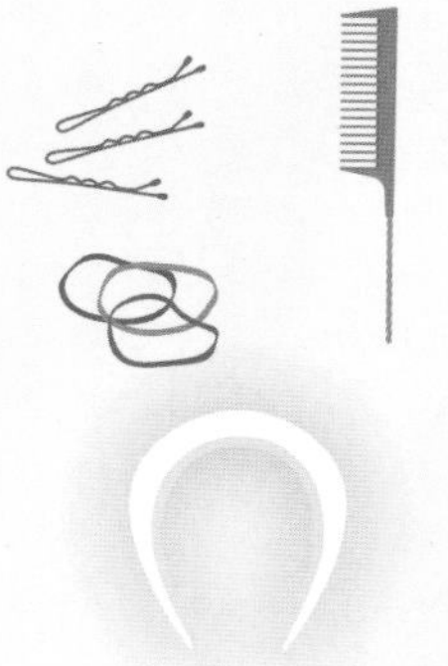

1 Start with straight hair with ends curled inward.

2 Using a rat-tail comb, section off 2-inch sections of hair to frame the face.

5 Bring the left braid over to the right. If you have short hair, simply pin in place.

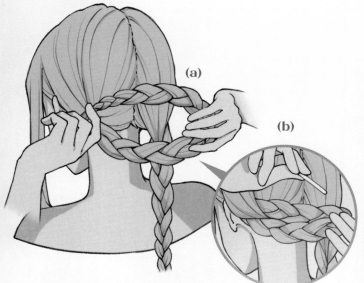

(a)

(b)

6 If you have longer hair, fold the braid in half under itself to make it shorter (a). Pin in place (b).

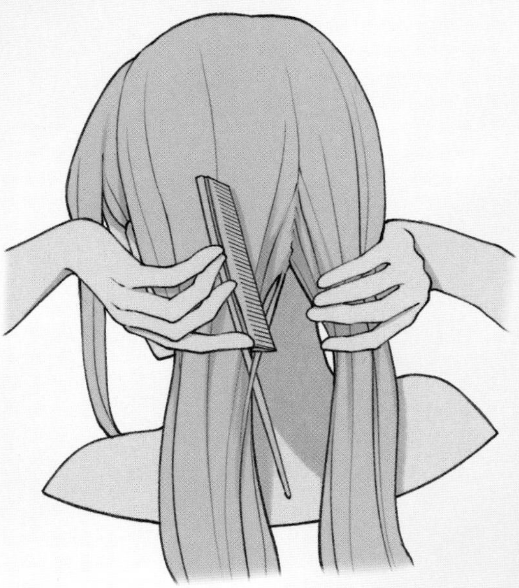

3 Split hair down the center with a rat-tail comb.

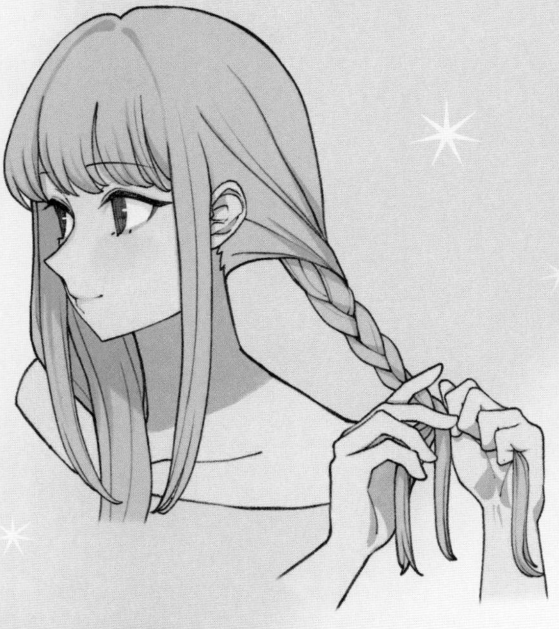

4 Braid each side into a three-strand braid. Secure with elastics.

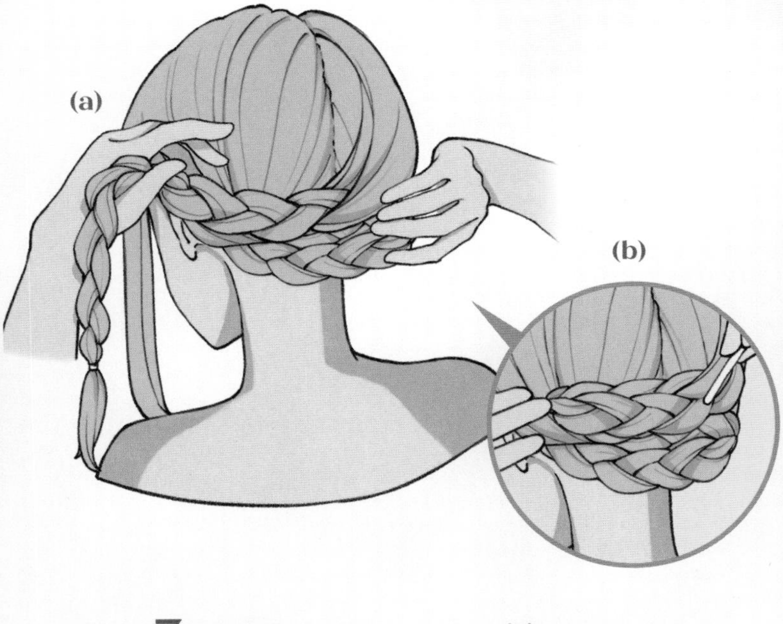
(a)
(b)

7 Repeat with the right braid, bringing it over to the left (a) and pinning in place (b) to create a braided crown effect.

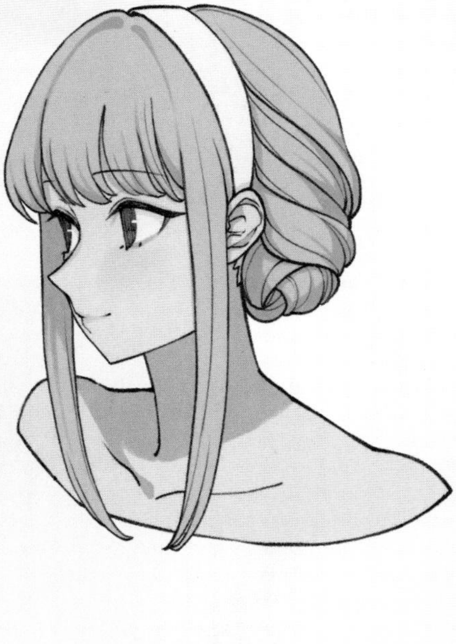

8 Finish with a headband.

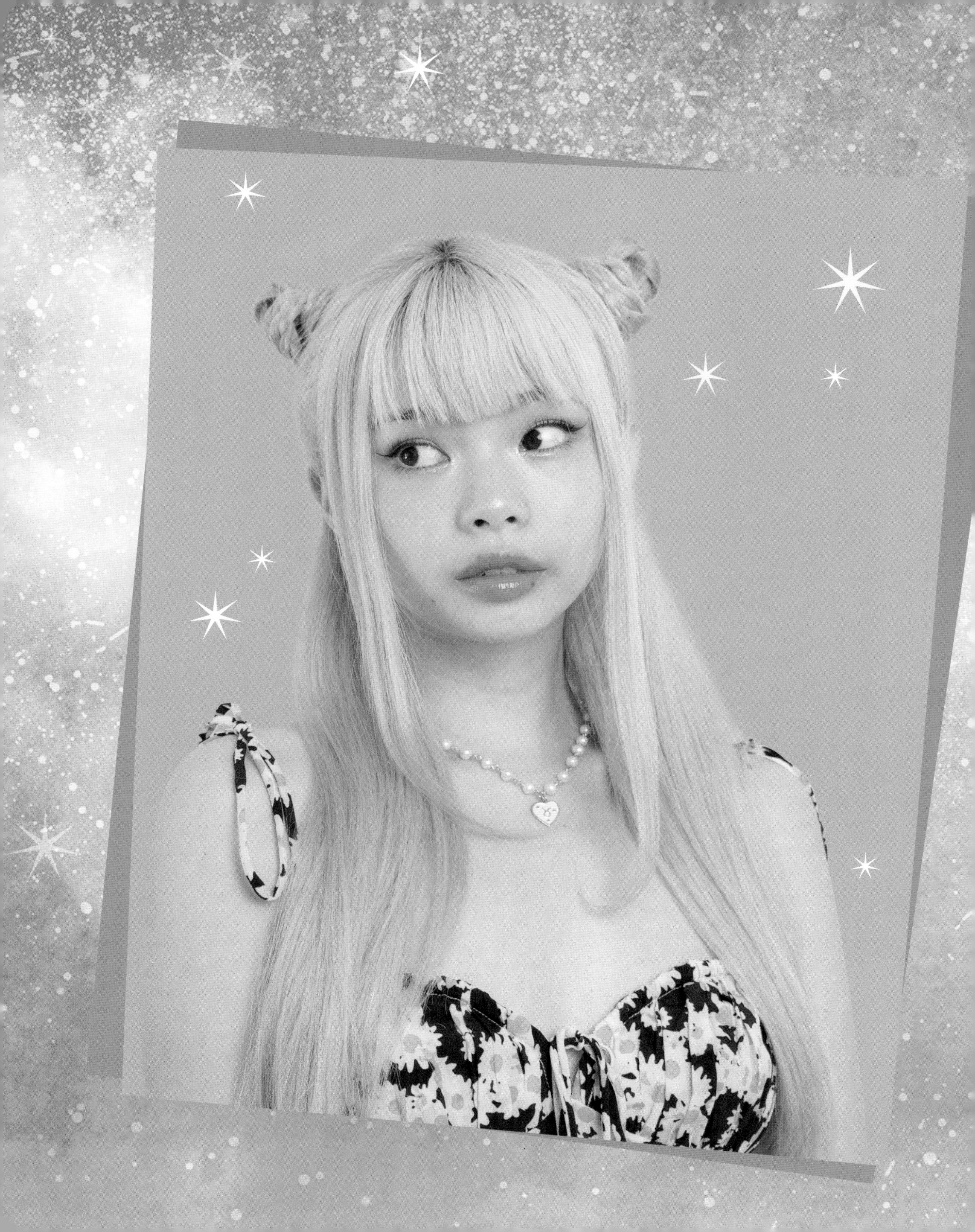

Anya

Spy x Family

When you run into the problem of not having the right hair accessory on hand, my favorite solution is to create it yourself! Anya Forger is the most adorable character and mascot from *Spy x Family*. She wears little horn-shaped hair clips on the top of her head, and these will serve as inspiration for this look. Using your own hair, you can create little horns to subtly reference Anya's hairstyle. It takes a little bit of practice to get the perfect horn shape, but it's easy once you get the hang of it!

Tools

Rat-tail comb
• Elastics • Bobby pins
• Hair spray

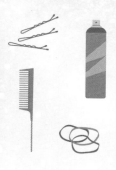

1 Start with straight hair with the ends curled in.

2 Using a rat-tail comb, section off two 1-inch sections to frame the face.

5 Twist the rest of the 2-inch braid tightly around the base. Bring the braid to the tip of the hair horn and wind the hair tightly around the tip, then looser around the base to create a horn shape. Bobby pin in place.

6 Wrap the remaining 1-inch braid around the base of the horn.

(b)

(a)

3 Gather two high pigtails and secure with elastics.

4 Braid each high pigtail into two braids: one 2-inch braid and one 1-inch braid (a). Using the 2-inch braid, pinch upward to create a 2-inch-tall base (b).

7 Bobby pin in place and spray with hair spray to keep secure.

Usagi

Sailor Moon

It's impossible to write an anime-inspired hairstyle book without including arguably the most iconic female character, Usagi from *Sailor Moon*. The *Sailor Moon* franchise is so successful that it's captured the hearts of fans all around the world, even beyond anime fans! This look layers different techniques that we've learned throughout this book to create her stunning double bun and twin tail updo. This look will have heads turning on the street.

I've done a variation of this look for my YouTube channel, but this reimagined tutorial brings us to a closer, more character-accurate representation. The new added use of multiple hairstyling tools helps recreate the different textures and curls in Usagi's bangs and pigtails.

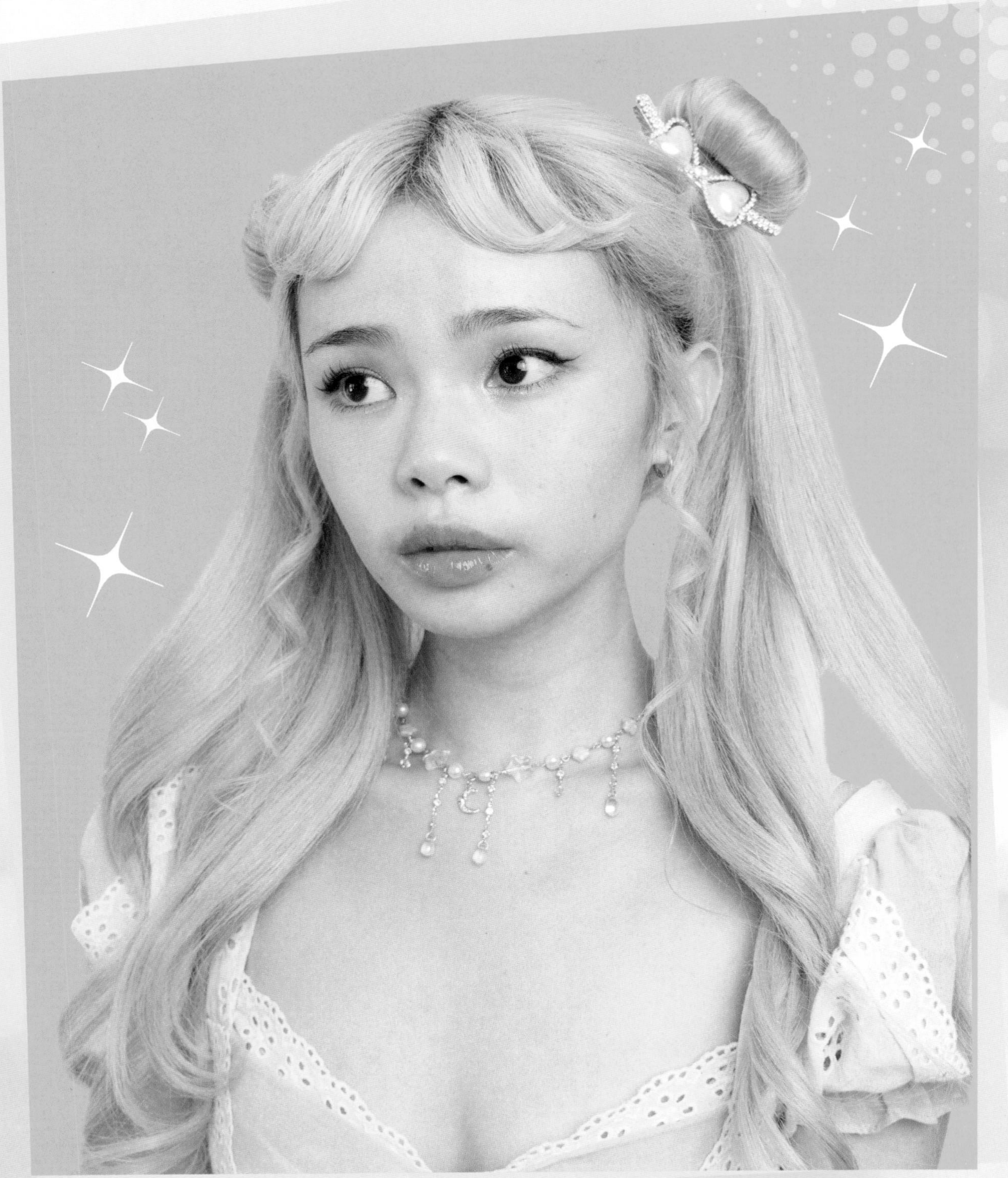

Tools

Elastics • Two small bun makers • Bobby pins • ½-inch-barrel curling wand • Flat iron • 1½-inch-barrel curling iron • Hair spray • Bejeweled clips

1 Start with straight hair.

2 Start with hair in two high pigtails. Secure with elastics.

4 Curl a micro-section of hair above the ears with a ½-inch curling iron.

5 Curl bangs inward using a flat iron. For those who don't have bangs, you can simply skip this step, or try clip-on bangs as an alternative.

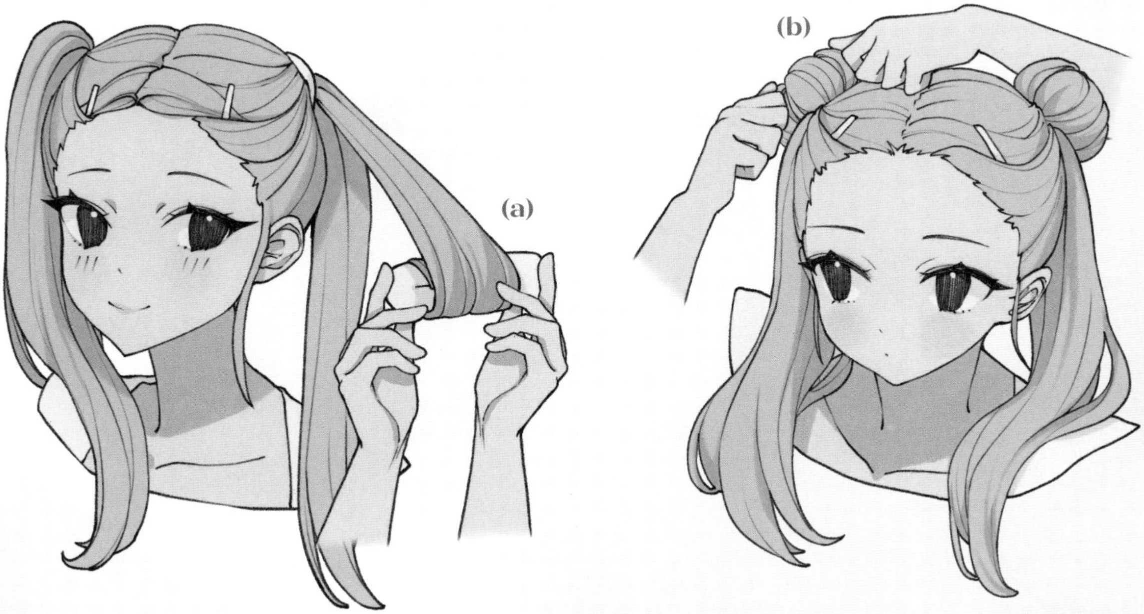
(a)
(b)

3 Section one-third of each pigtail and use that section to create two small buns using bun makers (a). Bobby pin in place (b).

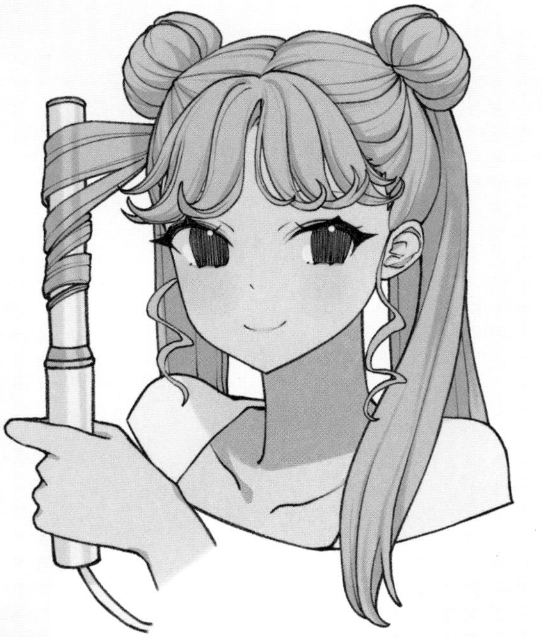

6 Loosely curl the ends of each pigtail with a 1½-inch-barrel curling iron.

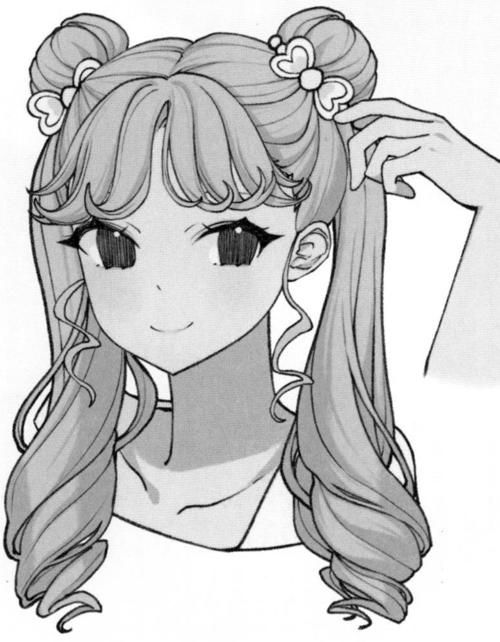

7 Spray with hair spray and accessorize with bejeweled clips to finish.

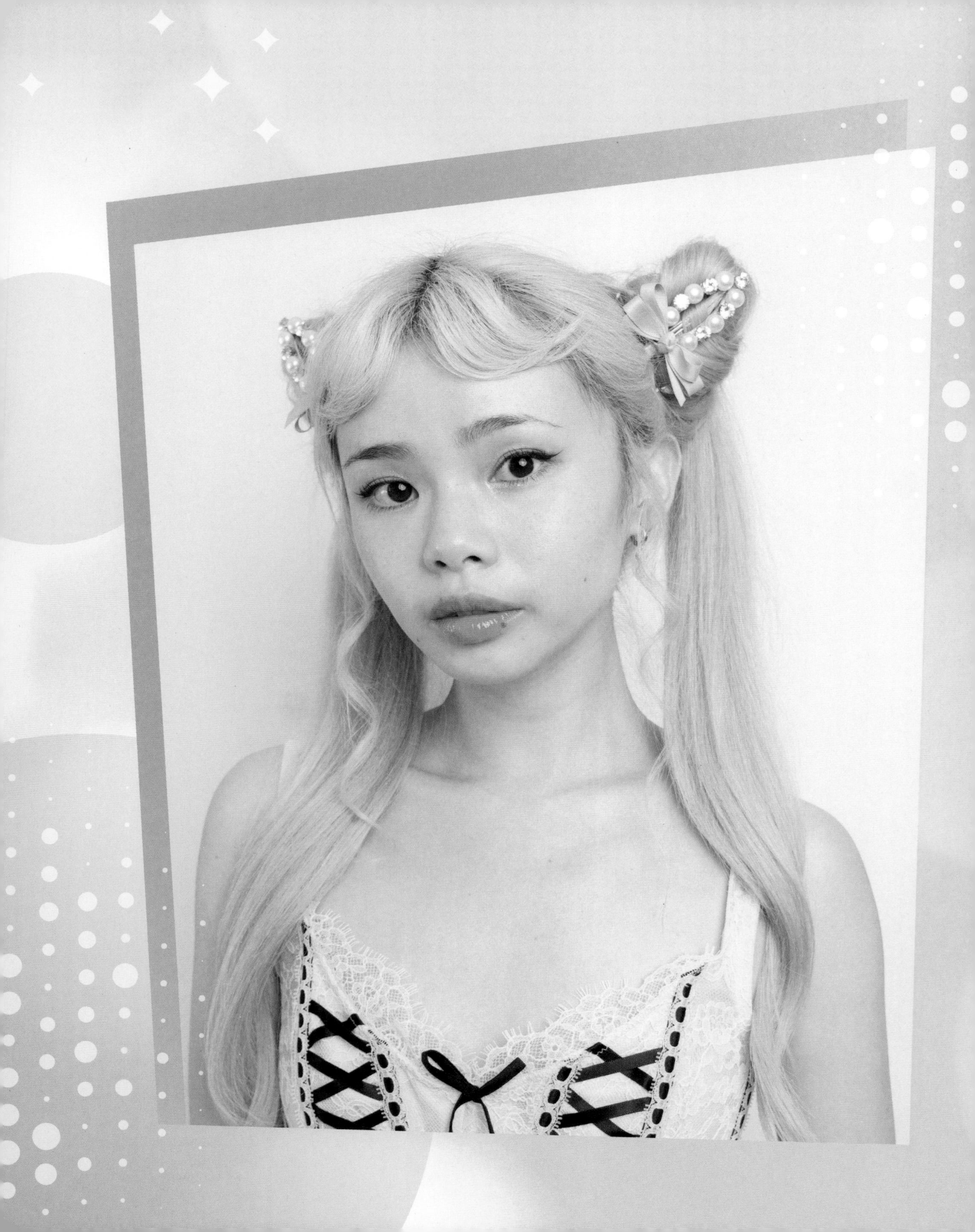

Chibi Usa

Sailor Moon

By this point in the book, you've probably become very familiar with the classically round bun. If you're looking for something more unique, Chibi Usa from *Sailor Moon* wears an interesting pointed bun that's reminiscent of a pair of rabbit ears. The same bun makers we've used before can be used to create a different hair shape—even these!

Tools

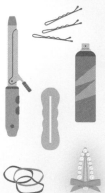

½-inch-barrel curling
wand • Elastics • Two
large bun makers •
Bobby pins • Hair spray
• Pearl hair clips

1 Start with loosely curled hair
and curled bangs. (For the
bangs, reference the Usagi
from *Sailor Moon* tutorial,
page 99, using a ½-inch-barrel
curling wand.)

2 Tie two high pigtails and
secure with elastics.

4 Instead of creating a flat donut shape
with the bun maker, pinch in half
vertically to create a horn-shaped bun.

(a)

(b)

3 Section half of each pigtail (a) to create two large buns using bun makers (b).

5 Stand the bun vertical and bobby pin in place.

6 Spray with hair spray and accessorize with pearl hair clips.

Tsuyu Asui

My Hero Academia

At first glance, Tsuyu Asui's hairstyle from *My Hero Academia* may look intimidating and incredibly complex, but with a simple hair-looping tool, you can easily create bows out of your own hair! Use this technique for a Tsuyu-inspired hairstyle, or let your imagination run wild and design something unique and adorned with bows. It's the perfect little addition for any hairstyle, especially when you're lacking in hair accessories. Why not create your own?

For ease of creating this hairstyle, I prefer to do a low side ponytail rather than one in the back, so you can see the process of creating the ribbon.

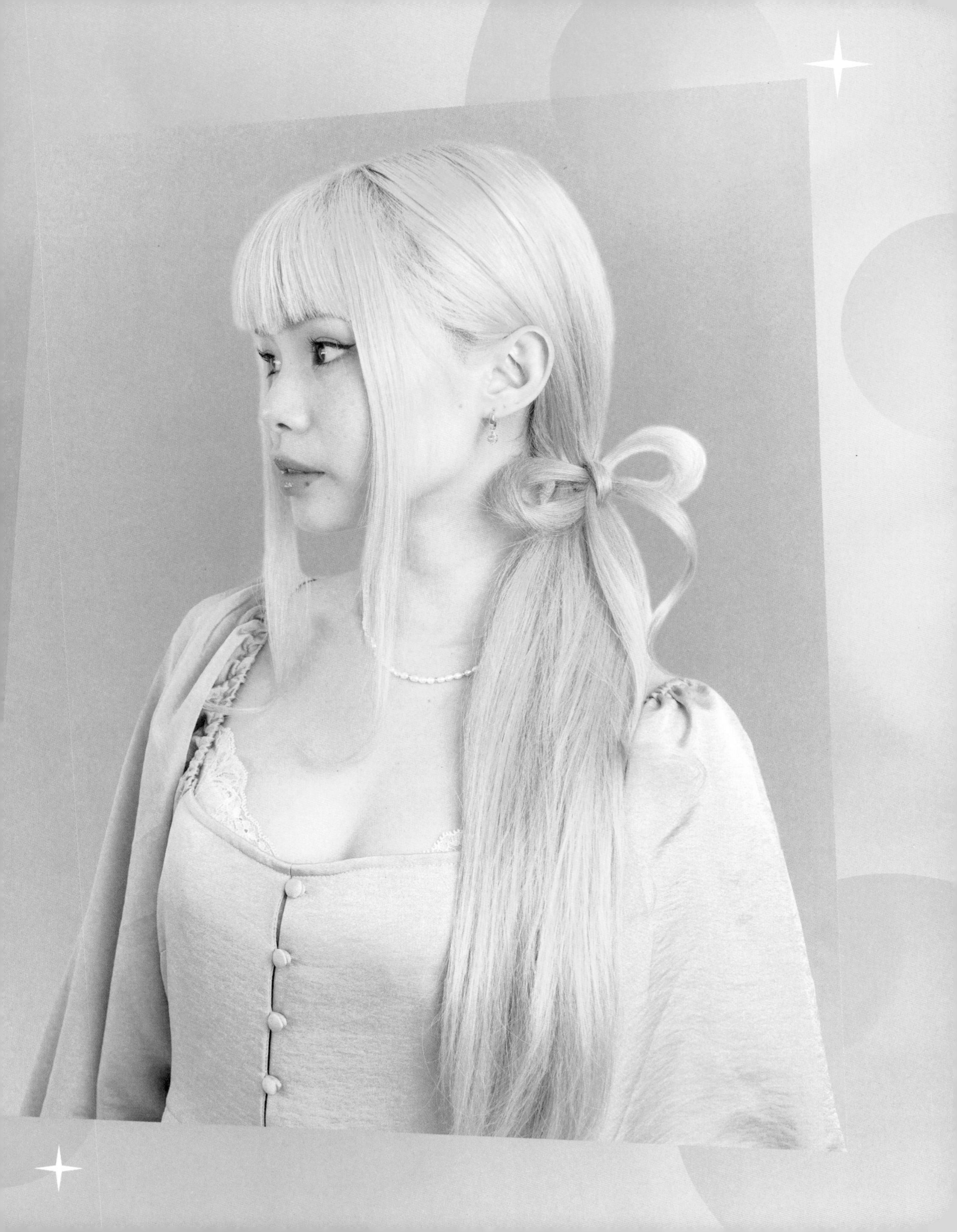

Tools

Rat-tail comb • Elastics • Hair-looping tool • Hair spray

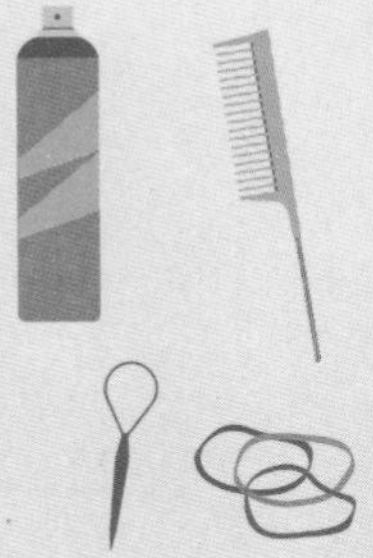

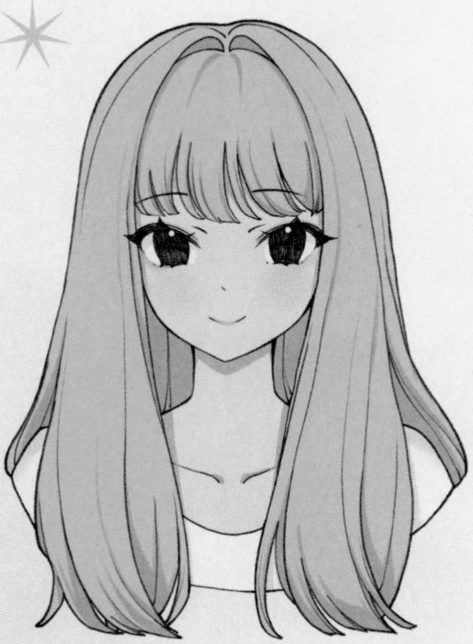

1 Start with straight hair.

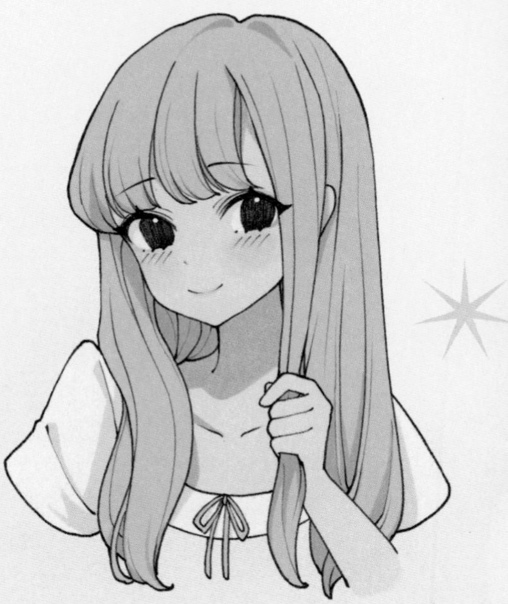

2 Using a rat-tail comb, section off 2-inch sections of hair to frame the face.

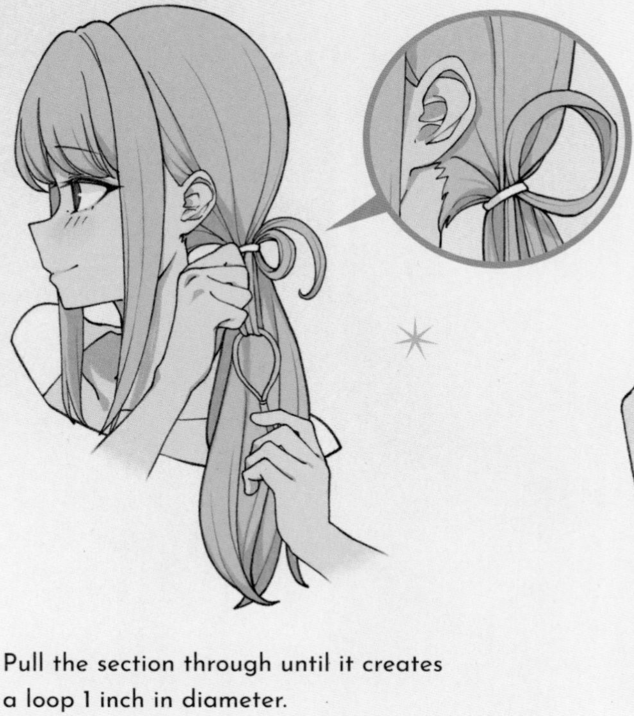

5 Pull the section through until it creates a loop 1 inch in diameter.

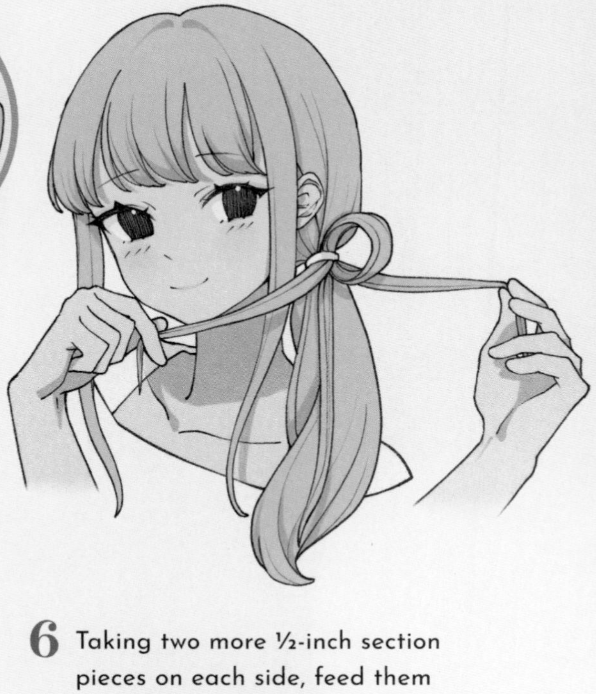

6 Taking two more ½-inch section pieces on each side, feed them through the middle loop to create the loops of a ribbon.

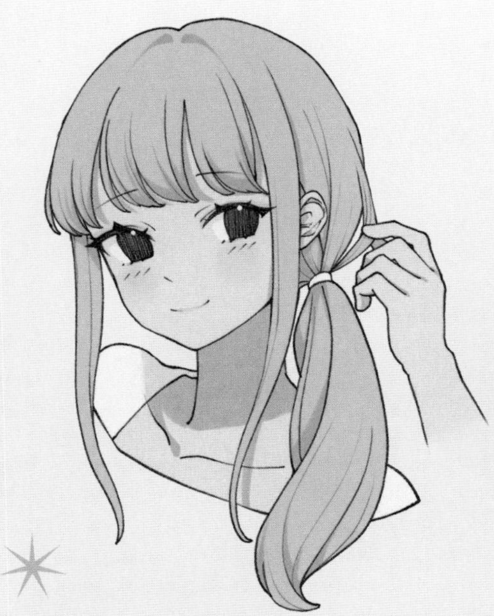

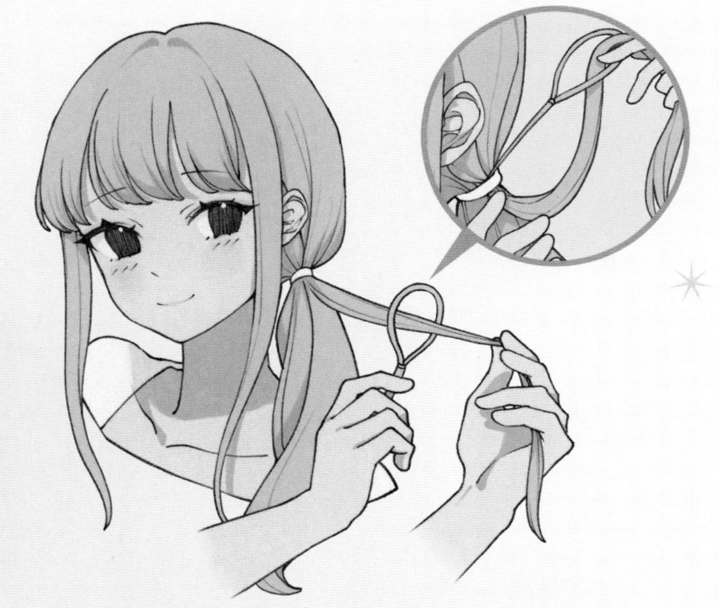

3 Gather the rest of the hair into a low ponytail and tie with an elastic. Gently loosen the ponytail with fingers.

4 With a hair-looping tool, create a large bow. Start by taking a ½-inch section of hair and feeding it through the looping tool.

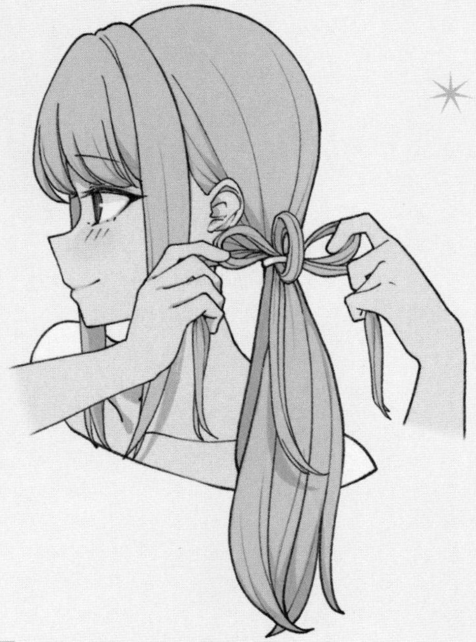

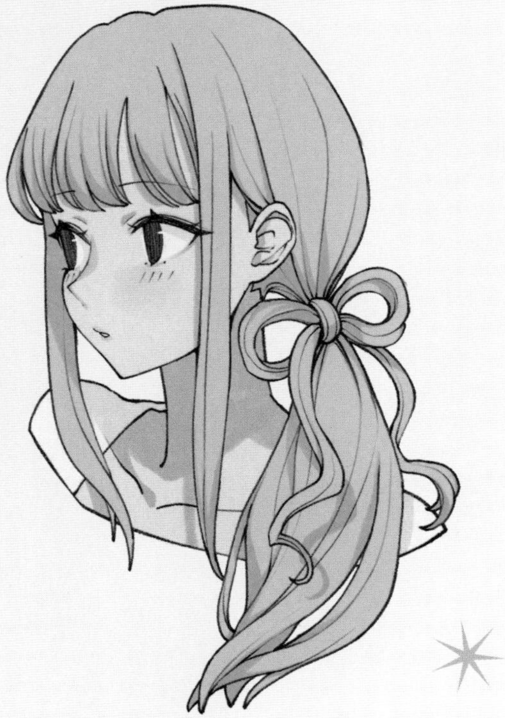

7 Pull the middle loop taut to secure the ribbon in place and spray with hair spray to hold.

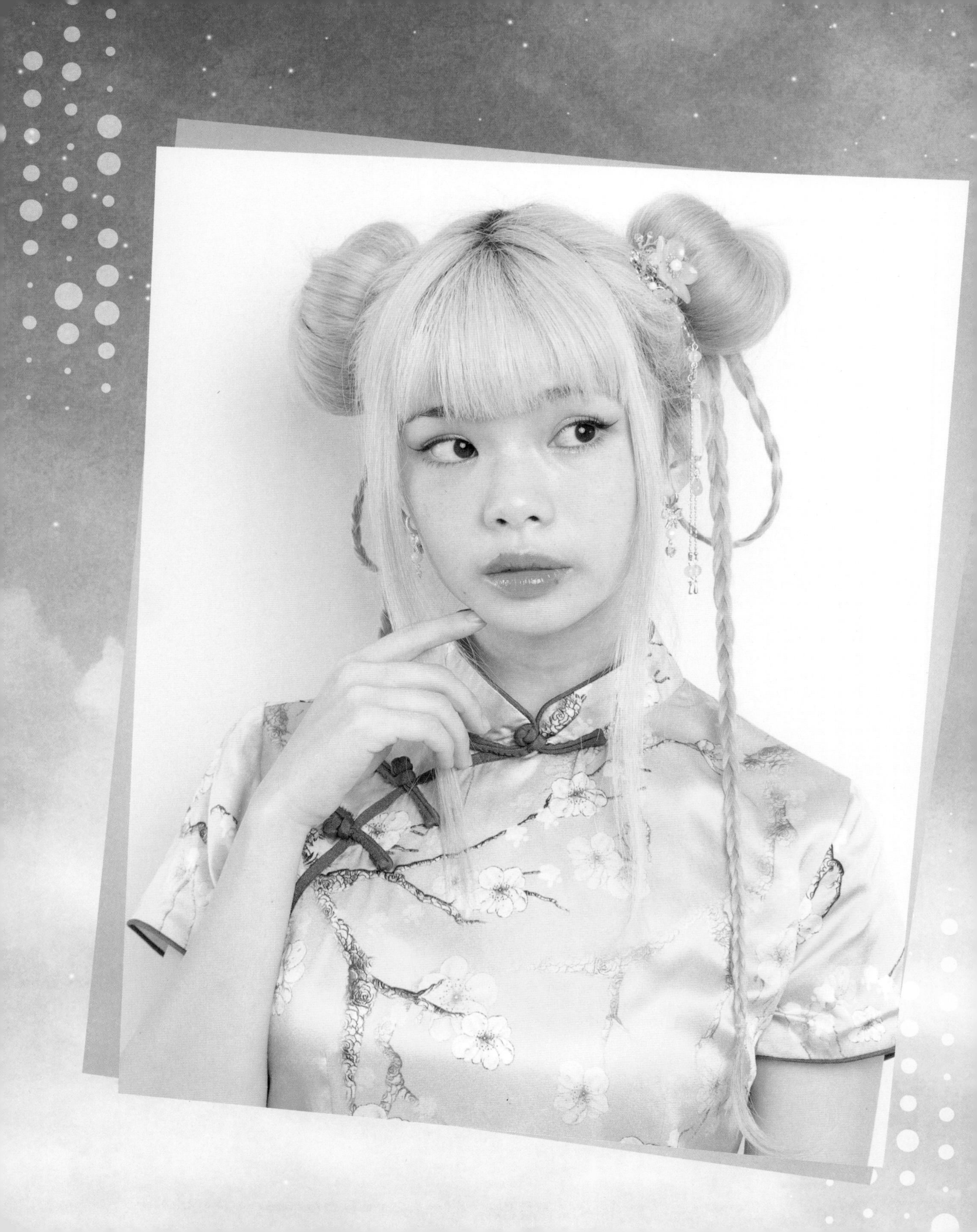

Ran-Mao

Kuroshitsuji

As mentioned earlier in this book, some of my favorite styles to recreate are from Chinese characters in anime. They tend to have highly decorated hairstyles adorned with intricate accessories, like Ran-Mao from *Kuroshitsuji*. Her hairstyle instantly captured my attention as a look that I wanted to recreate for a fun challenge. It looks complicated at first glance, but it is actually quite easy to recreate, once you break it down into multiple, easy-to-manage techniques. For this look, I've swapped out her double hair horns with fluffy buns instead for wearability.

Tools

Rat-tail comb • Elastics • Two large bun makers • Bobby pins • Hair spray • Floral hair clip with dangling tassel

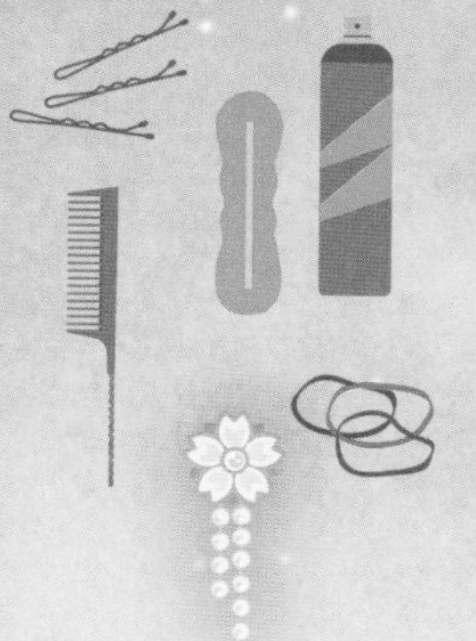

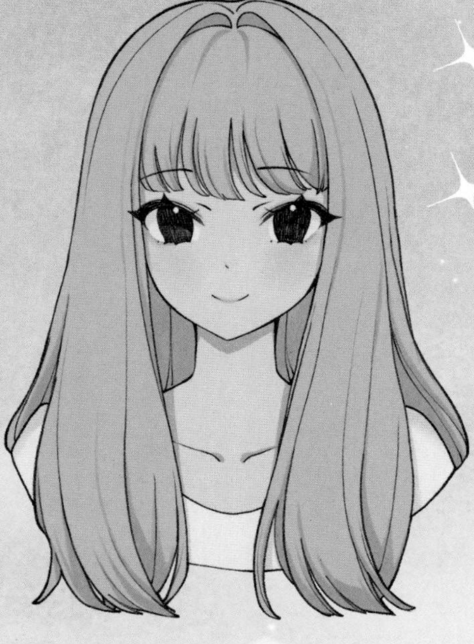

1 Start with straight hair.

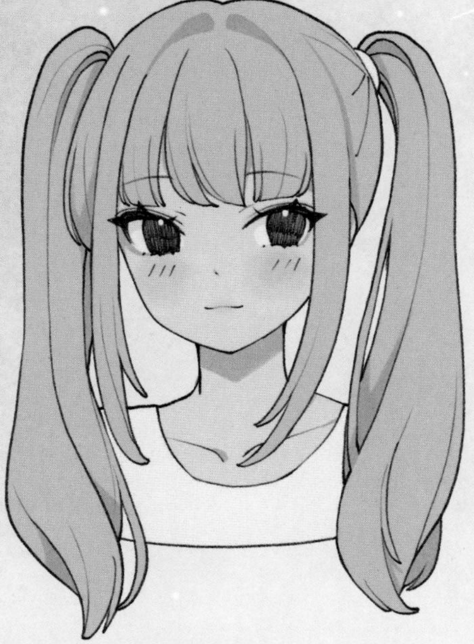

2 Using a rat-tail comb, section off 2-inch sections to frame the face. Gather the rest of the hair into two high pigtails. Secure with elastics.

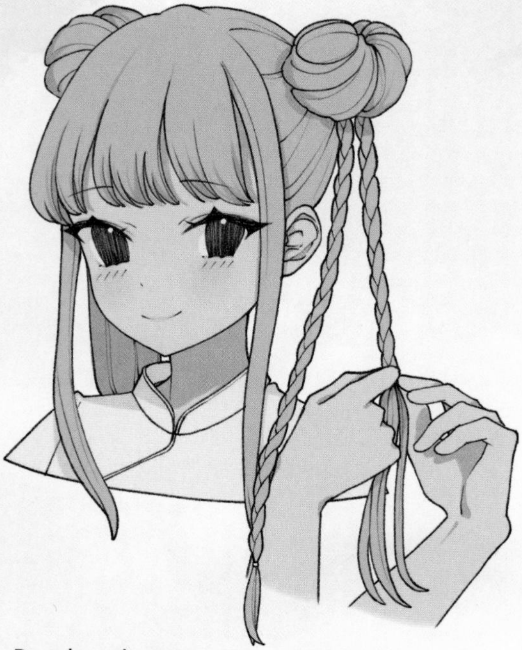

5 Braid each section into equal three-strand braids. Secure with elastics.

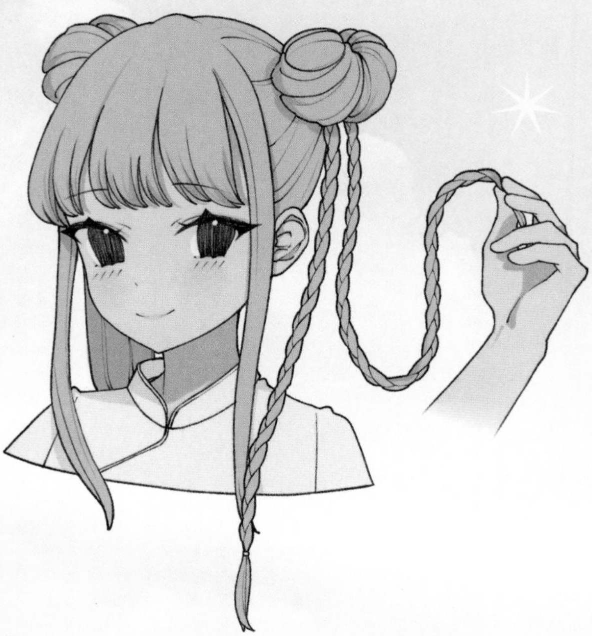

6 Take one of the braids on each side and create a loose chin-length loop.

3 Taking two-thirds of each pigtail, create a bun using a large bun maker. Bobby pin in place.

4 Split the remaining third of hair into two equal sections, then braid each section into equal three-strand braids. Secure with elastics.

7 Wrap the end of each braid around the base of the bun and bobby pin in place.

8 Spray with hair spray and accessorize with a floral hair clip.

Mitsuki Kouyama

Full Moon o Sagashite

Full Moon o Sagashite is one of the earliest manga
I remember picking up in elementary school. Because this
book is an homage to all the series that gave me childhood
inspiration, I knew I had to include Mitsuki Kouyama's hairstyle.
Her curly pigtails are accented by a braided crown in the
center, adding more texture and complexity to an otherwise
standard style. You can choose to create character-accurate
drill curls, as shown in the tutorial for Elizabeth Midford
(see page 61), or you can choose looser curls for daily
wearability, as I have in this demonstration. As always,
I encourage you to make changes to my tutorials as you see fit!

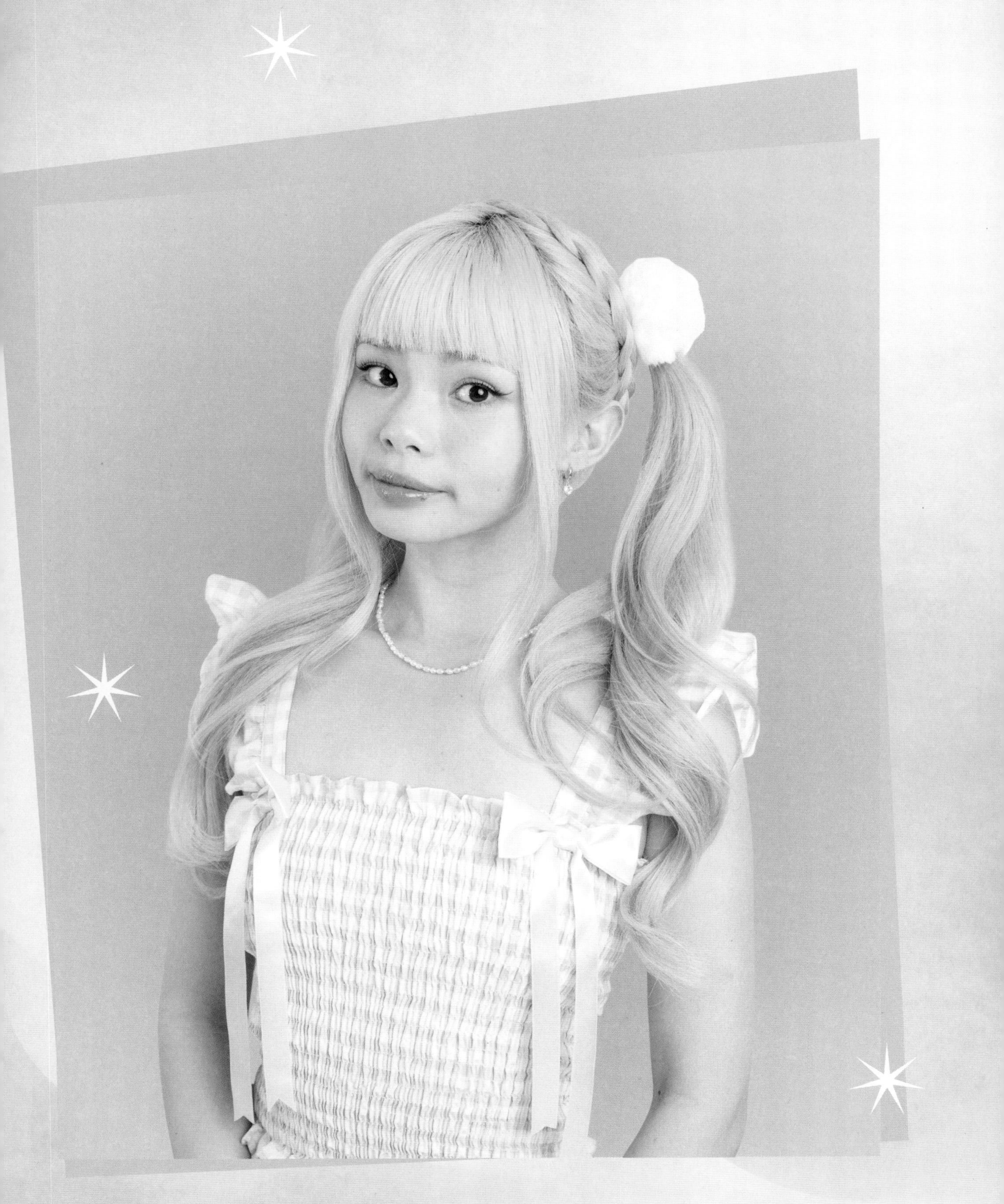

Tools

Rat-tail comb • Elastics • Bobby pins • Hair curling iron (1 inch for drill curls or 1½ inches for loose curls)

1 Start with straight hair.

2 Using a rat-tail comb, section off 1-inch sections of hair to frame the face.

5 Repeat steps 2 and 3 on the other side for a matching braid.

6 Because the braids were created in an upward motion, they should naturally lay across the top of the head. Lay the two braids neatly next to each other while tucking the loose end of each braid beneath the braid next to it.

3 Separate a 3-inch section of hair below the ear.

4 While guiding the hair upward, create a three-strand braid and tie with an elastic.

7 Bobby pin the braids in place behind the ears and discreetly along the braided crown for security.

8 Split the remaining hair into two even sections and tie into two high pigtails. Secure with elastics.

9 Curl the pigtails as desired.

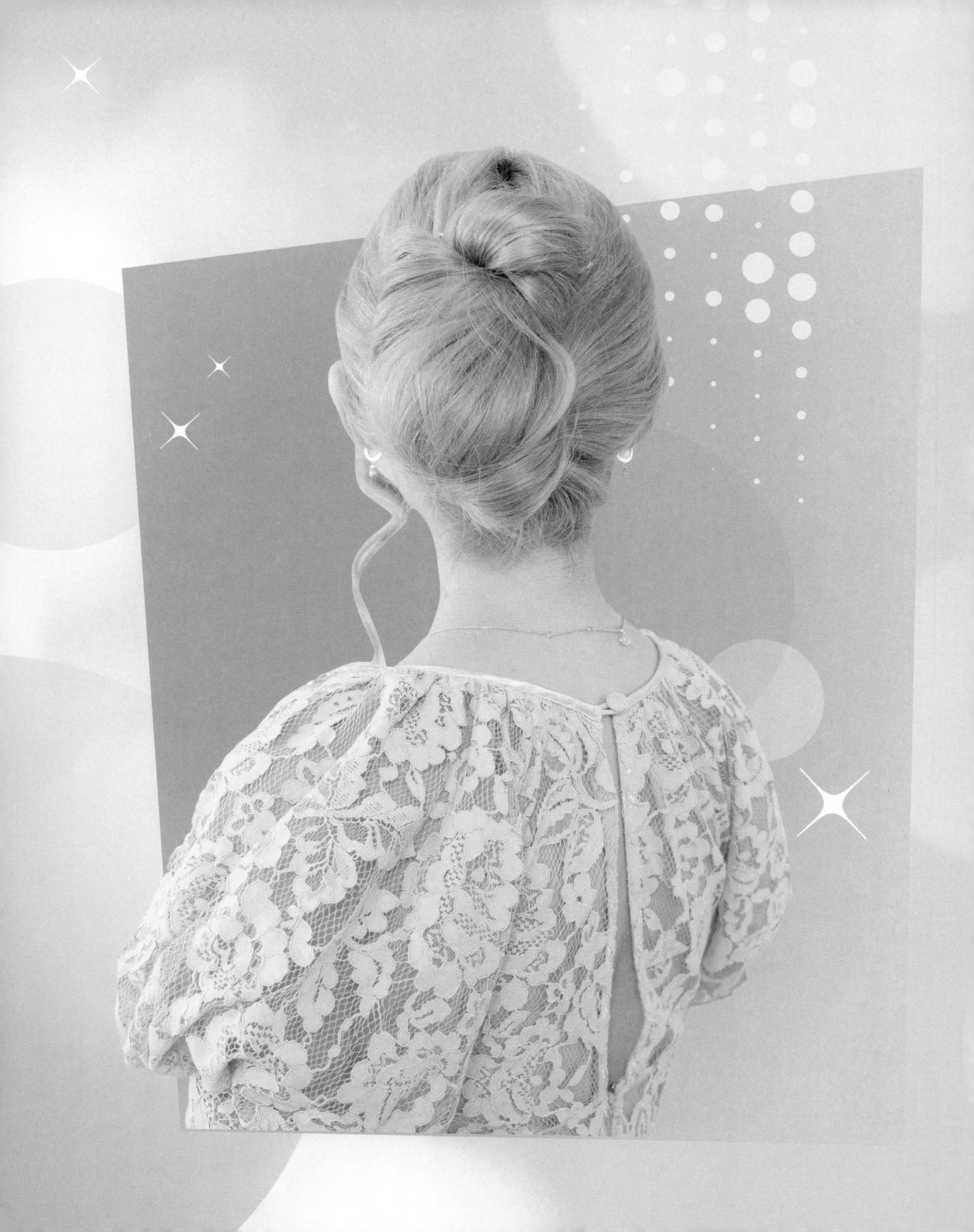

Blue Rose

Tiger & Bunny

For me, doing my makeup, putting on a great outfit, and doing my hair is almost like putting on armor to take on the world. Blue Rose from *Tiger & Bunny* does the same, changing from her plain brown hair to a stunning ice-blue updo when she fights crime. Although her updo looks complex, it's the perfect example of how even the most complicated anime hairstyles can serve as great inspiration for a simple, everyday look. When mastered, this easy French twist technique can take less than five minutes to do.

For your look, instead of a soda-drink-sponsored crown like Blue Rose wears in her superhero costume, why not top off your hairstyle with a sparkly crown instead?

Tools

Rat-tail comb
• Elastics • Bobby pins
• Hair spray

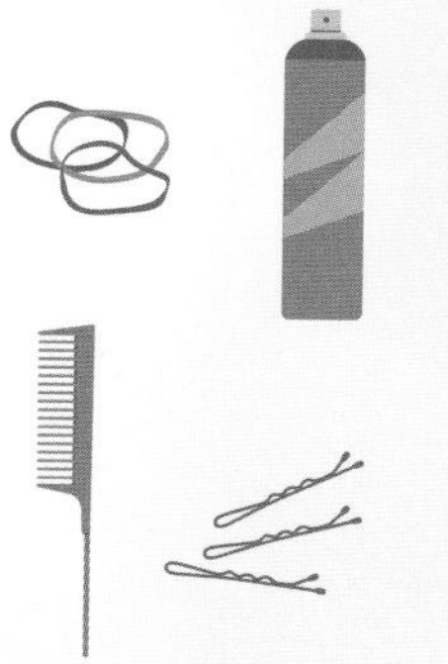

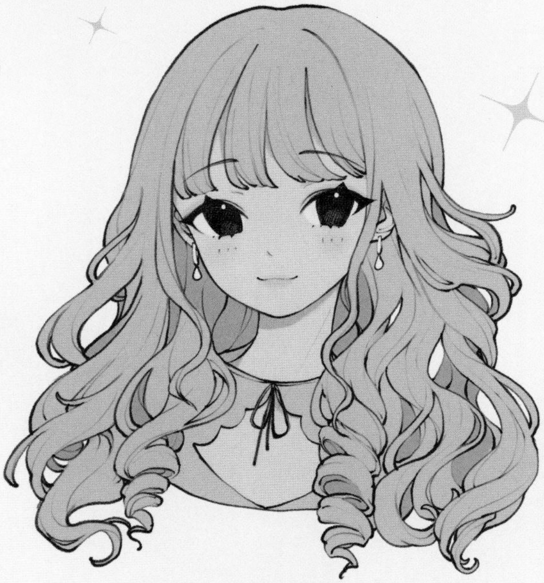

1 Start with curled hair.

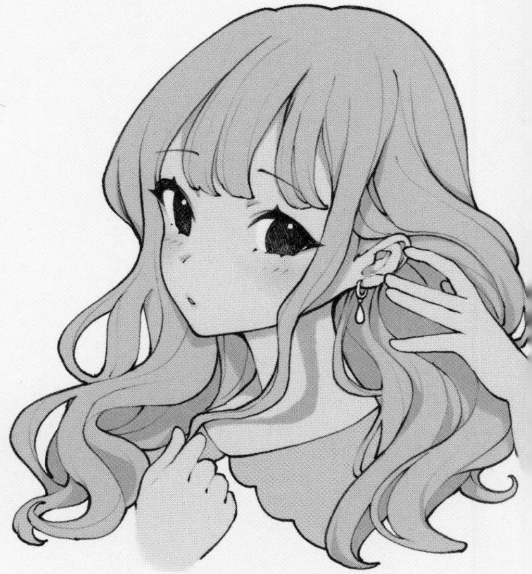

2 Using a rat-tail comb, section off 1-inch sections of hair to frame the face.

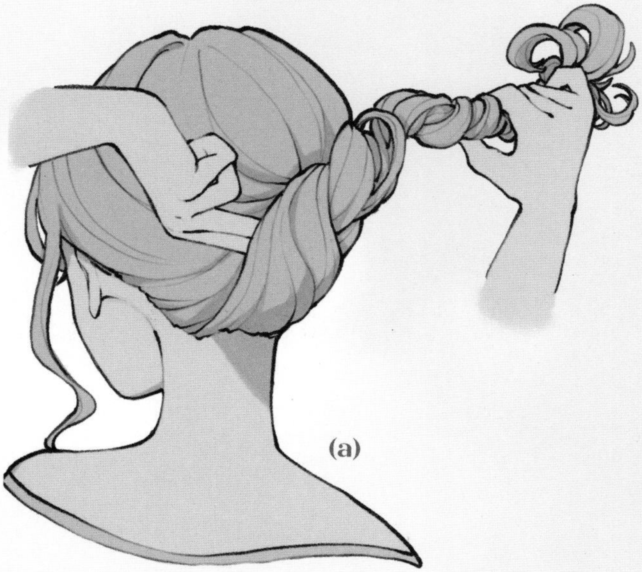
(a)

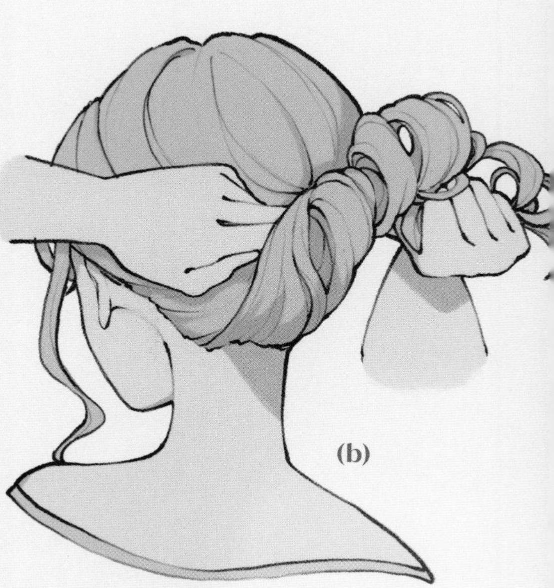
(b)

5 Wrap the twist around two fingers (a) and twirl, guiding the hair upwards (b).

3 Gather the rest of the hair into a loose, low ponytail, secure with an elastic.

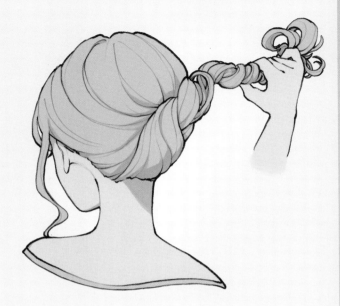

4 Twist the ponytail to the right side.

6 Loosen and maneuver the hair with fingers to hide the wrap and bobby pin into place.

7 Use hair spray to smooth any flyaways.

Biscuit Krueger

Hunter x Hunter ✦ High Ponytail

I've been inspired by anime since I was a kid, and *Hunter x Hunter* was one of my earliest favorites. I remember being in second grade, jittering with excitement, because I couldn't wait for elementary school to let out so I could go home and watch my favorite show. I can attribute a lot of my creativity to that time, too, as my personal style was influenced by creative looks I saw on-screen.

Biscuit Krueger, also known as Bisky, is a deceptively cute and young character from *Hunter x Hunter*, one of the most famous shounen (targeted to adolescent boys) anime. The series has run for more than twenty-five years, and it's one of the best-known series to date. Biscuit wears several looks throughout the series, with her high ponytail being one of the most iconic.

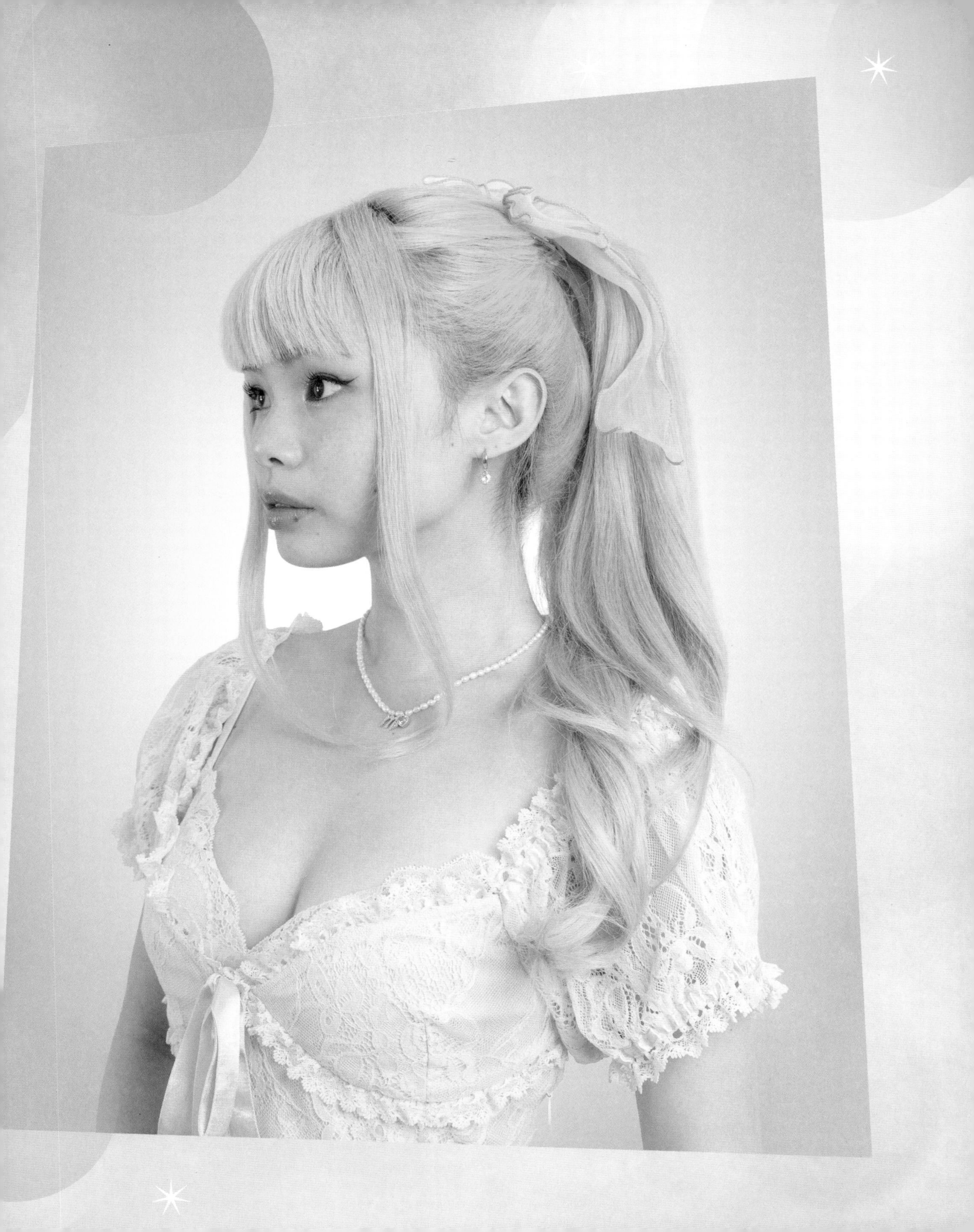

Tools

Rat-tail comb • Bobby pins • Elastics • Hair extensions • Hairbrush • Curling iron • Hair ribbon • Hair spray

1 Start with straight hair.

2 Using a rat-tail comb, section off 1-inch sections of hair at the front to frame the face.

(a)

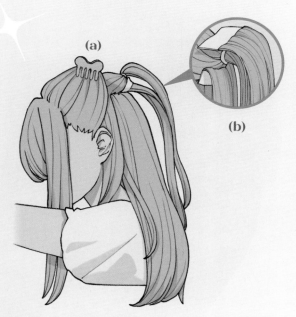

(b)

6 Bring the small ponytail to the front and section away for now (a). With another 2-inch-wide extension, clip on top of the small ponytail to create a ponytail sandwich (b).

7 Gather the remaining hair around the sandwich and tie in place to blend the length of the extensions. Optional: Repeat the process of sandwiching hair extensions around the small ponytail to create more volume and length.

3 Gather the top fifth of hair in the front and pin away for now.

4 Beneath that section, gather a 1-inch section of hair and tie with an elastic. (Imagine a small high ponytail.) Bring the small ponytail to the front and section away for now.

5 Take a 2-inch-wide extension, flip the small ponytail upside down, and clip in the extension beneath the small ponytail. Flip the small ponytail back down.

9 Gather the rest of the hair and brush to smooth into a high ponytail. Secure with multiple elastics.

10 Curl the ends of the ponytail with a curling iron.

11 Accessorize with a hair ribbon at the base of the ponytail to hide the elastics and spray with hair spray to hold.

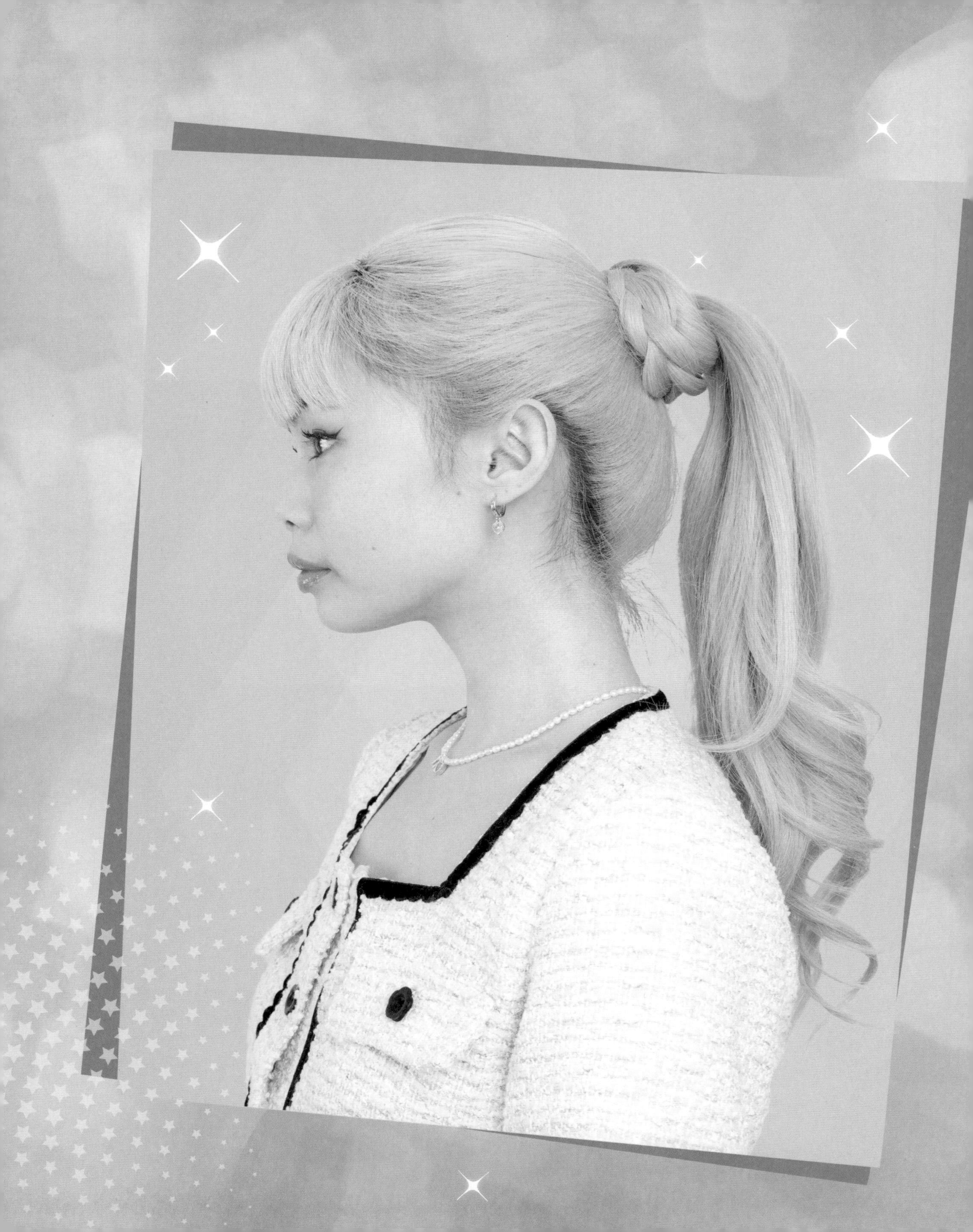

Biscuit Krueger

Hunter x Hunter ✦ Updo Version

Biscuit Krueger returns later in *Hunter x Hunter* with another adorable hairstyle. She sports a shorter updo surrounded by a thick braided crown, making this hairstyle easier to wear in warmer weather. When looking to anime characters for inspiration, I love looking at how the characters themselves wear their hair in different ways. The more looks they have, the more inspiration I get!

It's a bit difficult for me to tell whether she wears a ponytail or a bun, but I think either interpretation looks great. For this tutorial, I've chosen a simple high ponytail to mirror her usual style.

Tools

Hairbrush • Elastics
• Bobby pins
• Hair spray

1 Start with loose curls.

2 Start by pulling back all the hair into a tight, high ponytail. Use a hairbrush to gently smooth out flyaways and secure with an elastic.

4 Braid into a three-strand braid and tie with an elastic. Lightly loosen the braid for extra volume.

5 Gently wrap the braid around the base of the ponytail to hide the elastic.

3 Separate a 3-inch section of hair from the ponytail.

6 Bobby pin the braid in place and spray with hair spray to hold.

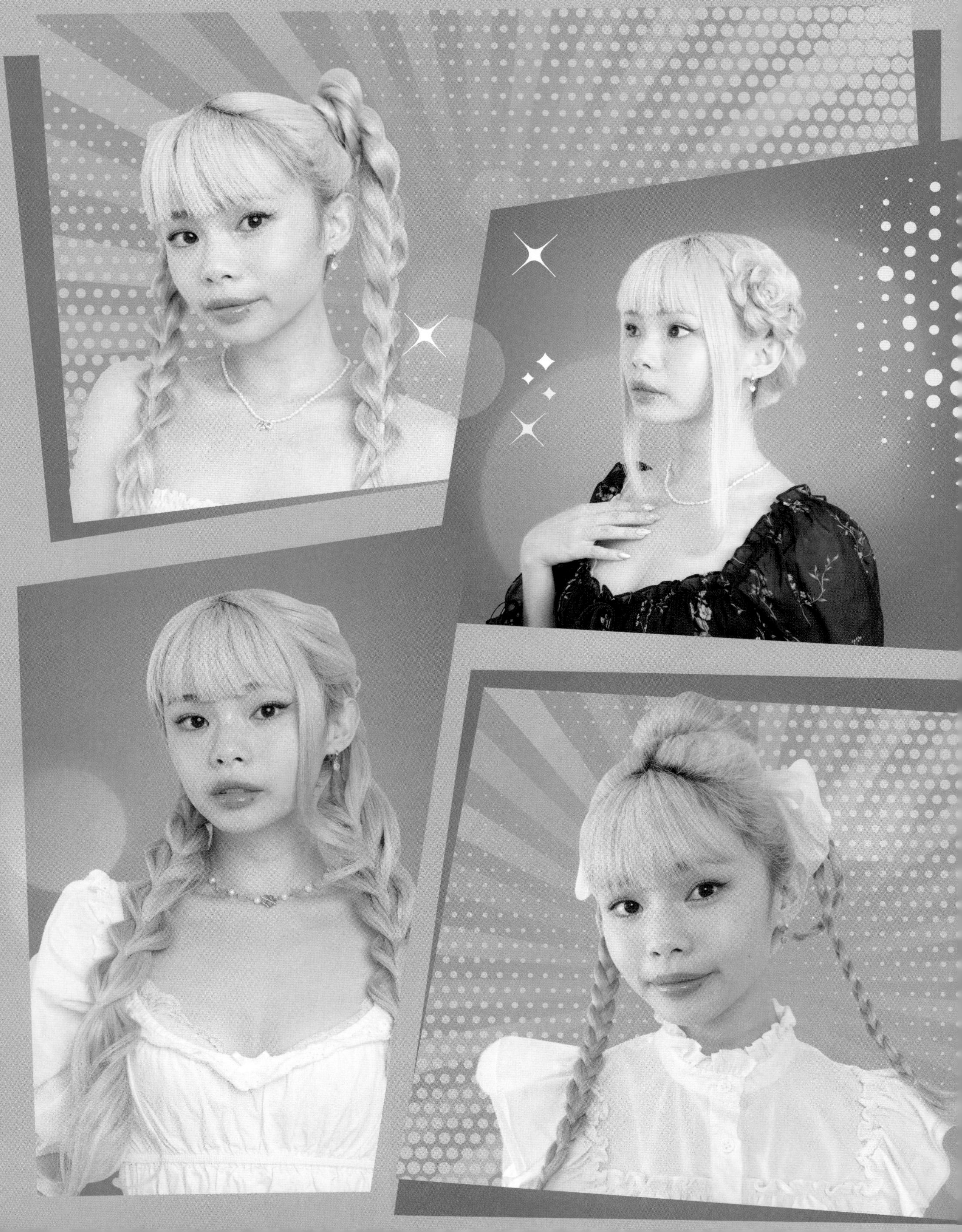

ADVANCED

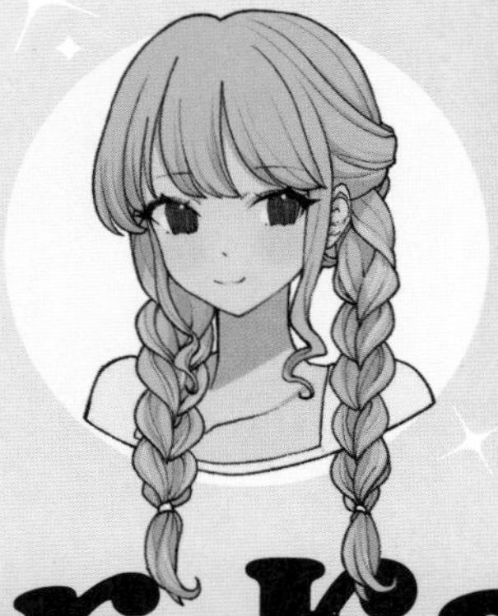

Mitsuri Kanroji

Demon Slayer

I'm no stranger to hair dye, but creating anime-inspired hairstyles has really encouraged me to work with color. Different-colored hair extensions allow the possibility of changing up your look on a whim, without the pressure of dyeing your hair. Mitsuri Kanroji from *Demon Slayer* gave me the idea to wear colored extensions that are longer than the natural hair length to give a pop of color. You could even change the colored extensions to match your look, giving you tons of possibility to play with this style!

Mitsuri wears three voluminous braids, with two on the side and one in the back. I've chosen to recreate her look with just two braids instead of three for more wearability.

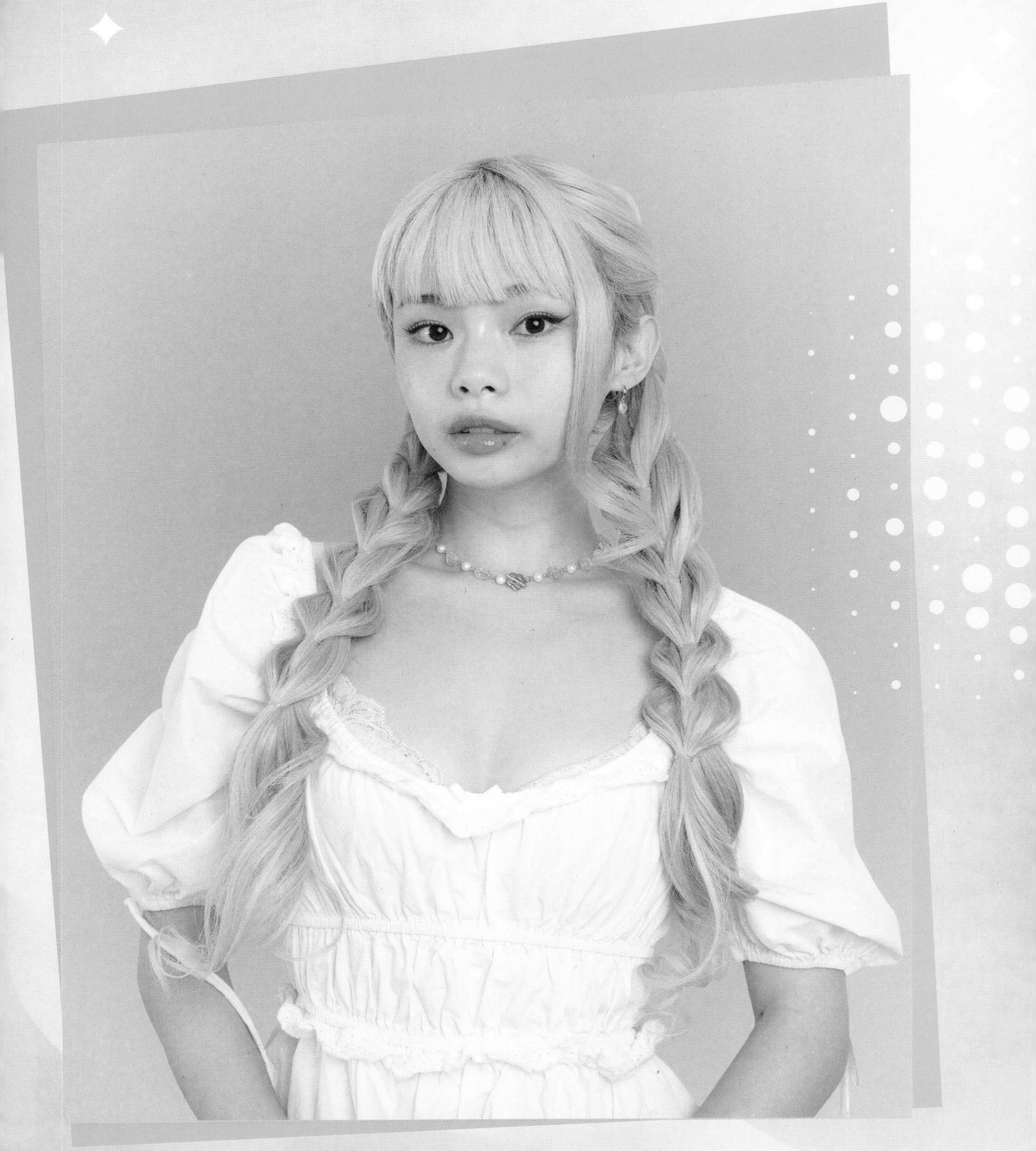

Tools

Hair extensions
• Rat-tail comb
• Elastics • Twisted loop

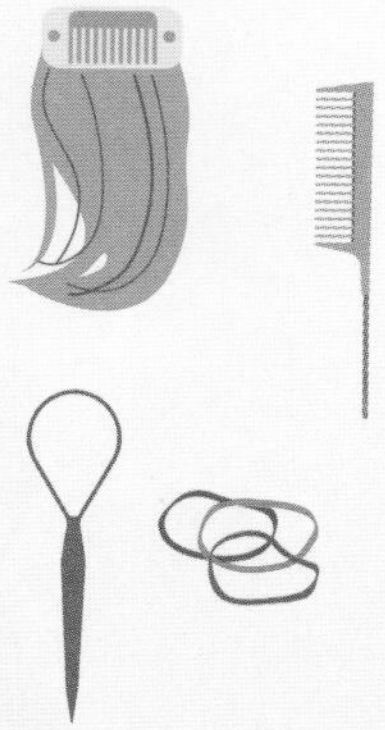

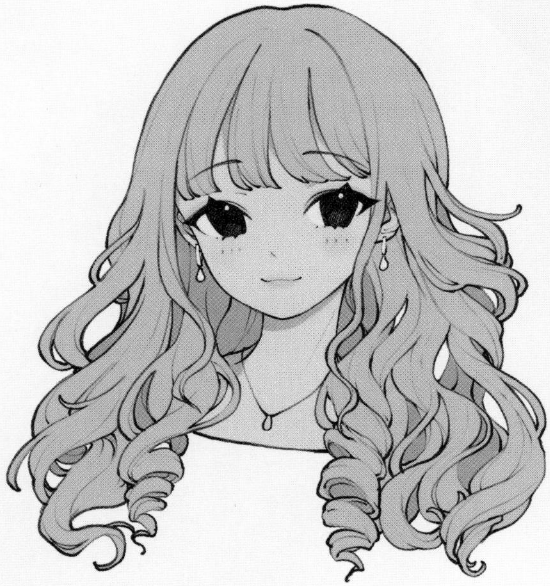

1 Start with curled hair, for volume.

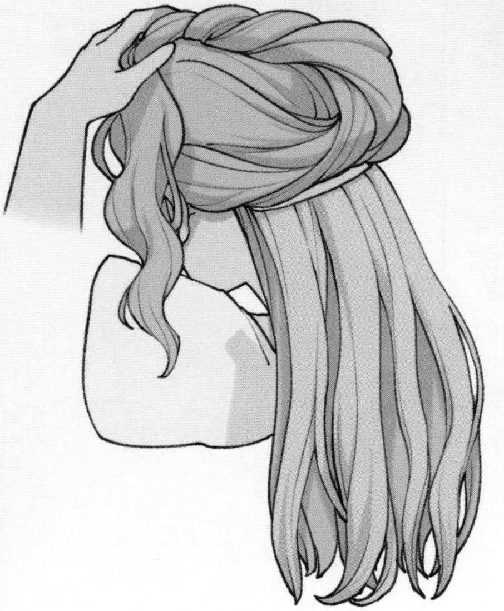

2 Add a full set of extensions slightly longer than your natural hair length and in a different color for a pop of color.

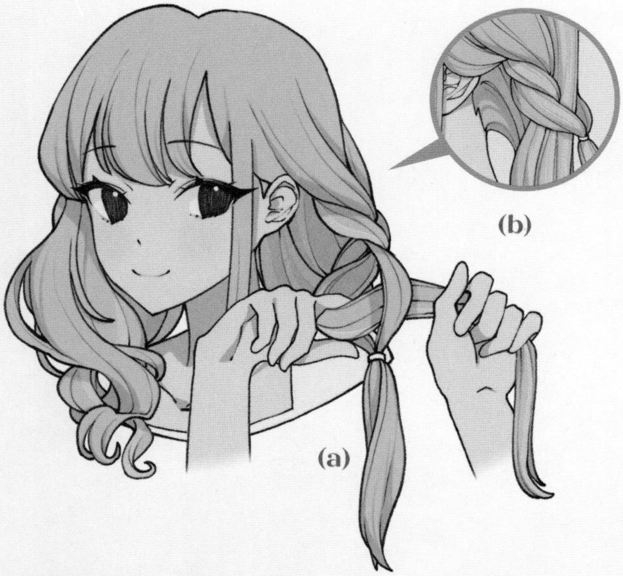
(b)
(a)

6 Feed half the hair through the twisted loop for a low pigtail (a). Tighten the loop (b). Lightly loosen the hair framing the face for volume.

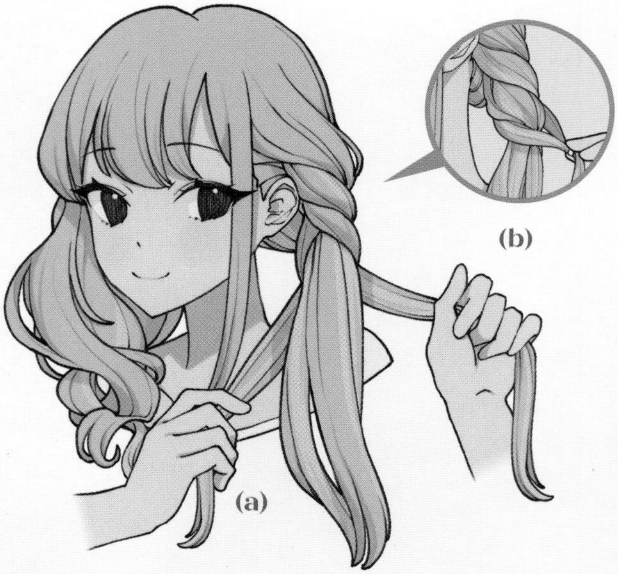
(b)
(a)

7 Create a faux fluffy braid by gathering 1-inch sections of hair on each side (a) and joining them in the middle (b), about 1 inch down from your starting position.

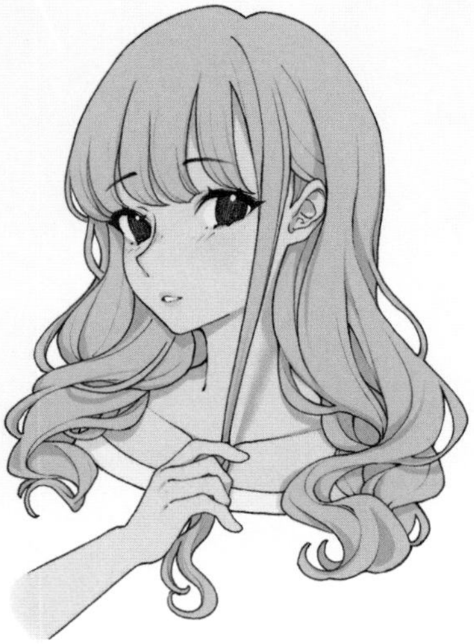

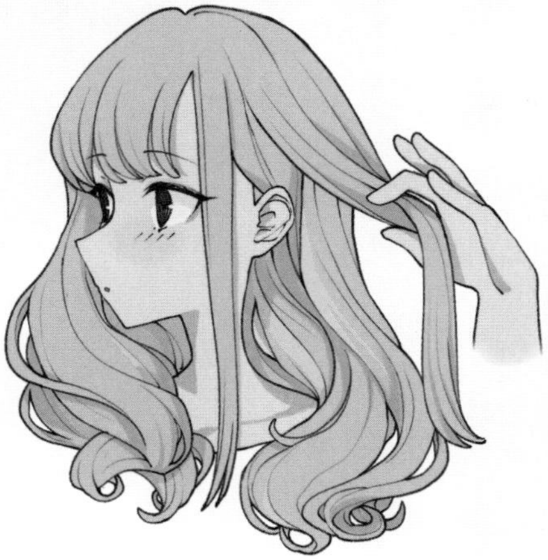

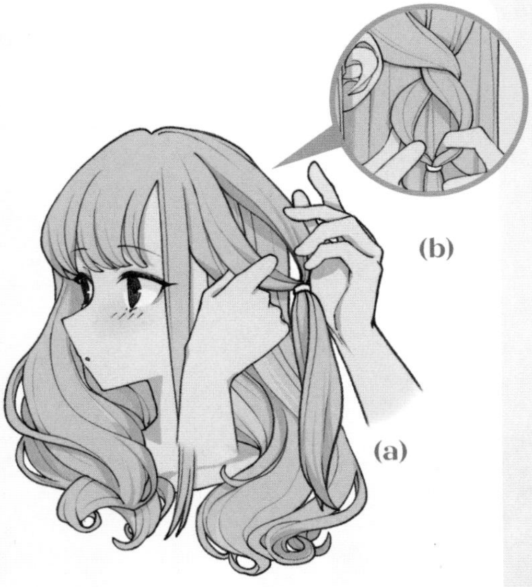
(b)
(a)

3 Using a rat-tail comb, section off a 1-inch section of hair to frame the face.

4 Gather a loose 3-inch section of hair above each ear and secure with an elastic.

5 Create a slit in the middle of the 3-inch section (a). Twist this section backward twice (b).

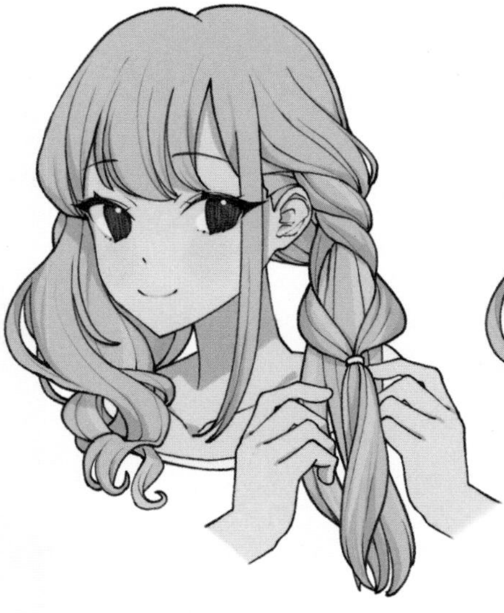

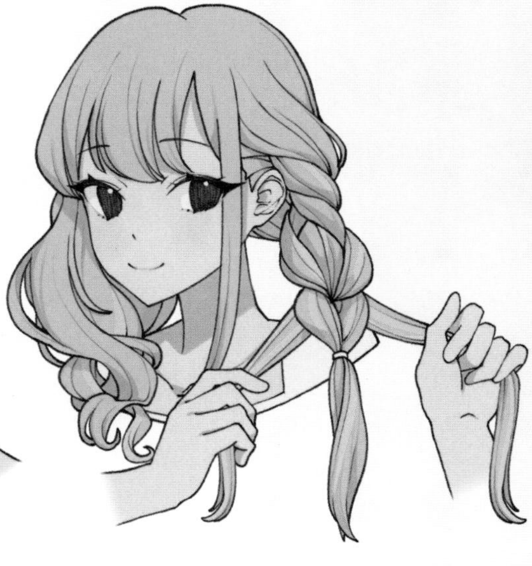

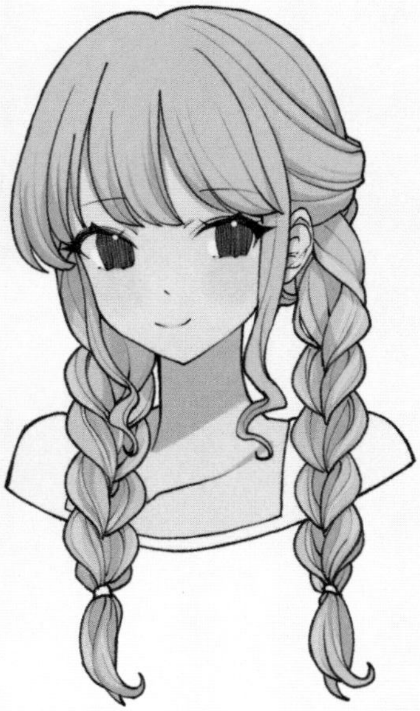

8 Secure with an elastic. Lightly loosen the hair with fingers for volume.

9 Repeat step 6 all the way down to the end of the braid, stopping a couple inches above the end of the hair.

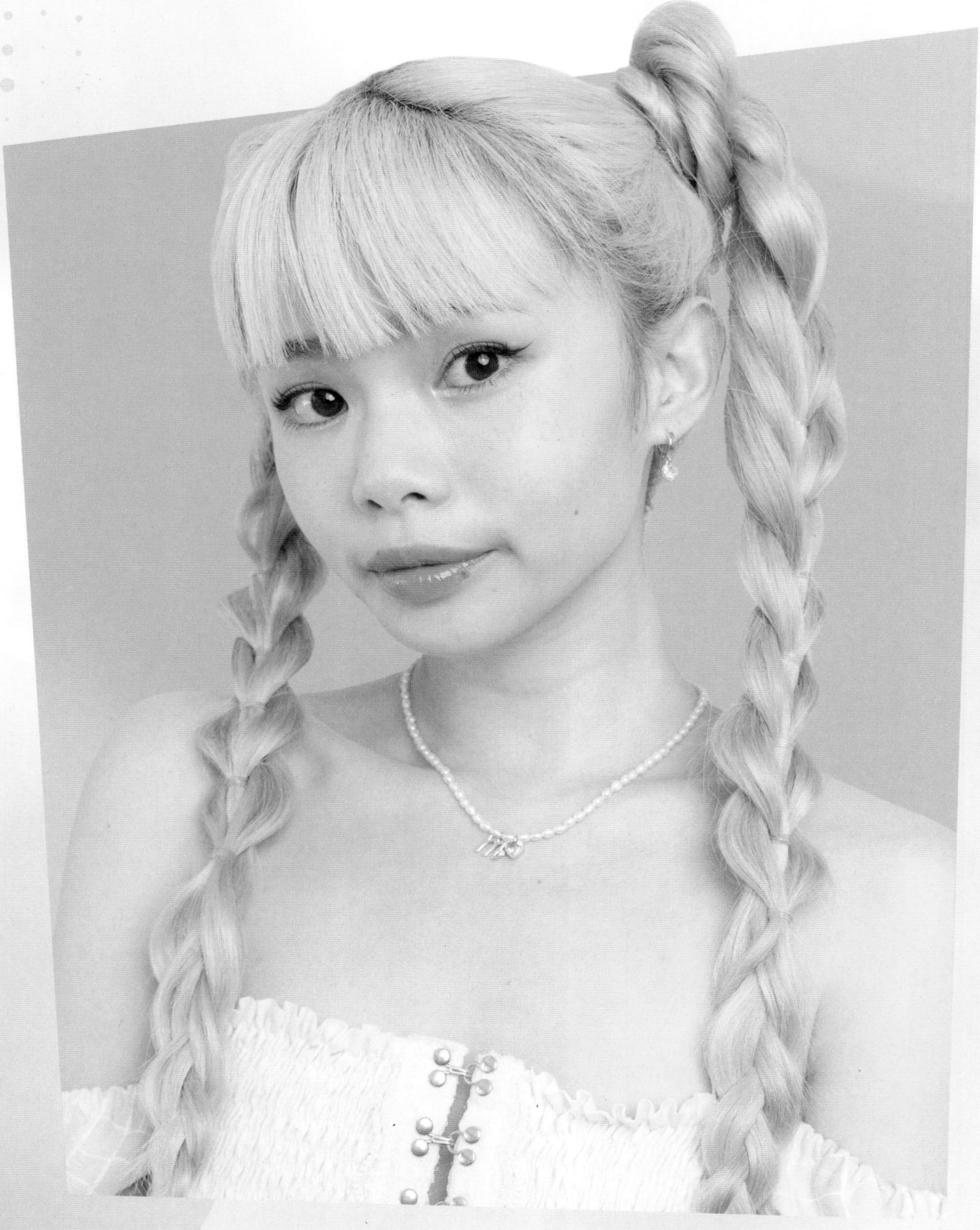

Sakurada Miwako

Paradise Kiss ◆ Voluminous Buns and Braids

The fourth and final style inspired by Miwako in this book is her voluminous double braids. This is personally one of my favorite styles in this book; if I could wear my hair like this every single day, I would!

Tools

Hair extensions
• Rat-tail comb
• Bobby pins • Elastics
• Hair spray

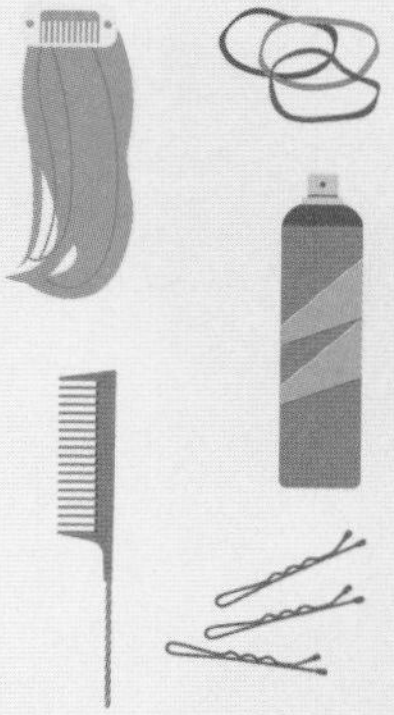

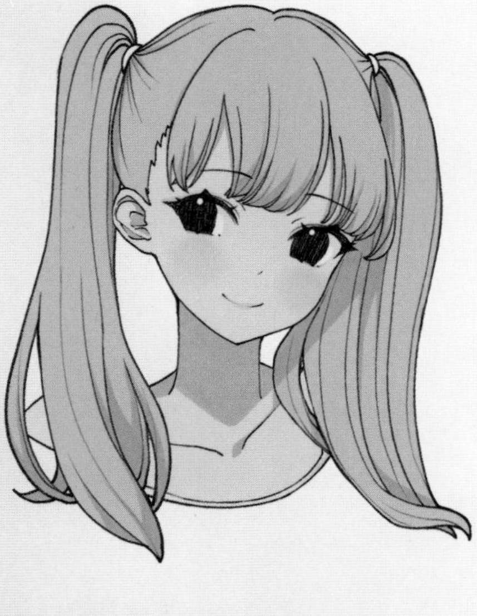

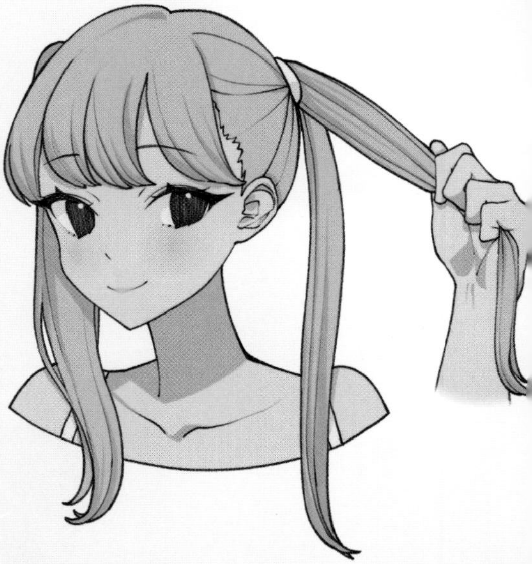

1 Start with double twin tails with extensions as shown in the tutorial for Sakurada Miwako's Twin Tails (see page 79).

2 Using a rat-tail comb, section off a 2-inch section of hair from the top of each pigtail and pin away for now.

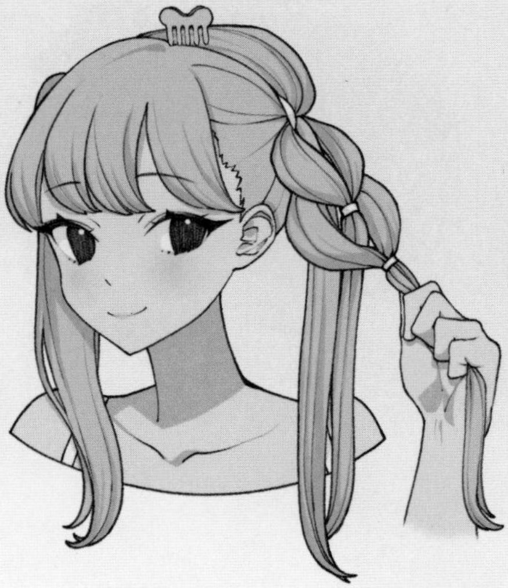

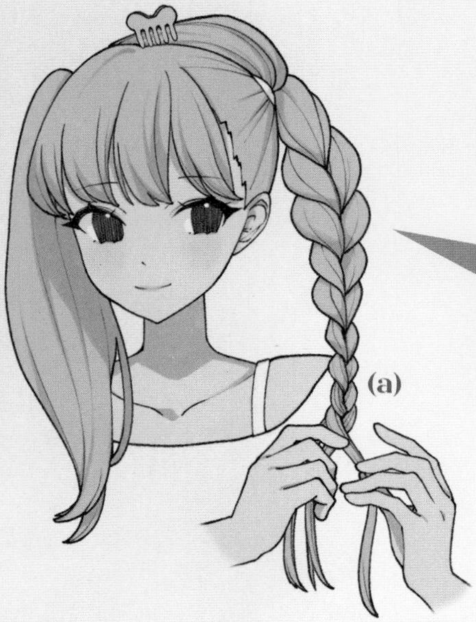
(a)

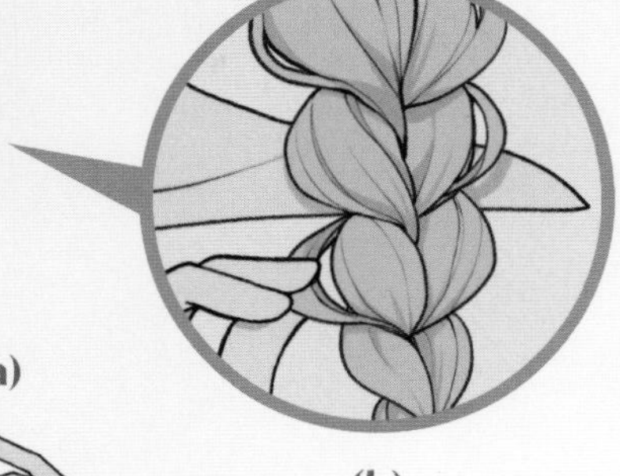

(b)

4 Repeat step 3 until close to the end of the pigtail.

5 When the hair starts to thin near the end, it becomes a bit difficult to create a faux braid. Finish off the braid with a regular three-strand braid instead (a).

6 Secure with an elastic. Gently loosen the braid for volume (b).

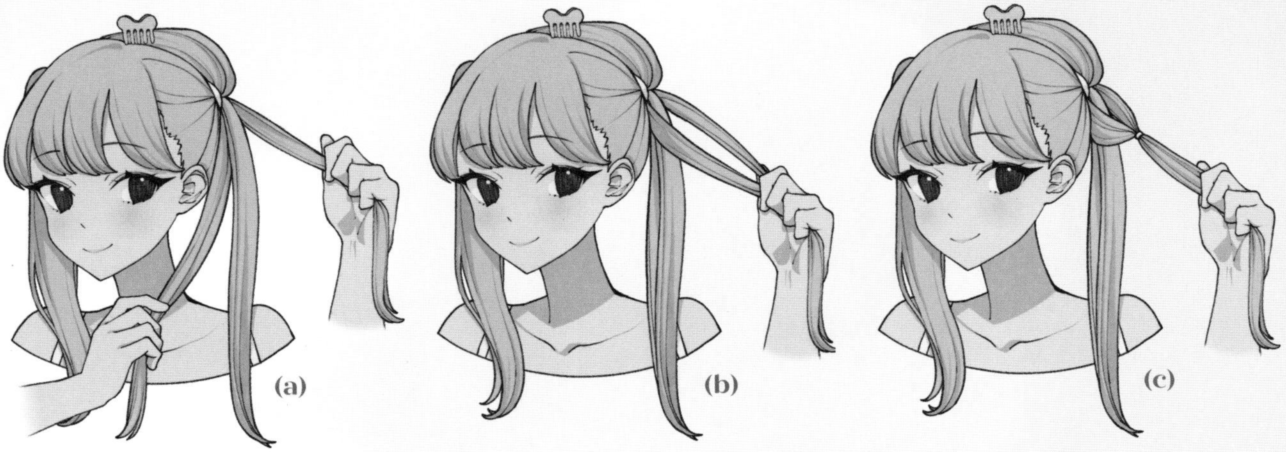
(a)
(b)
(c)

3 Create a faux fluffy braid by gathering 1-inch sections of hair on each side (a) and joining them in the middle 1 inch down from your starting position (b). Secure with an elastic (c).

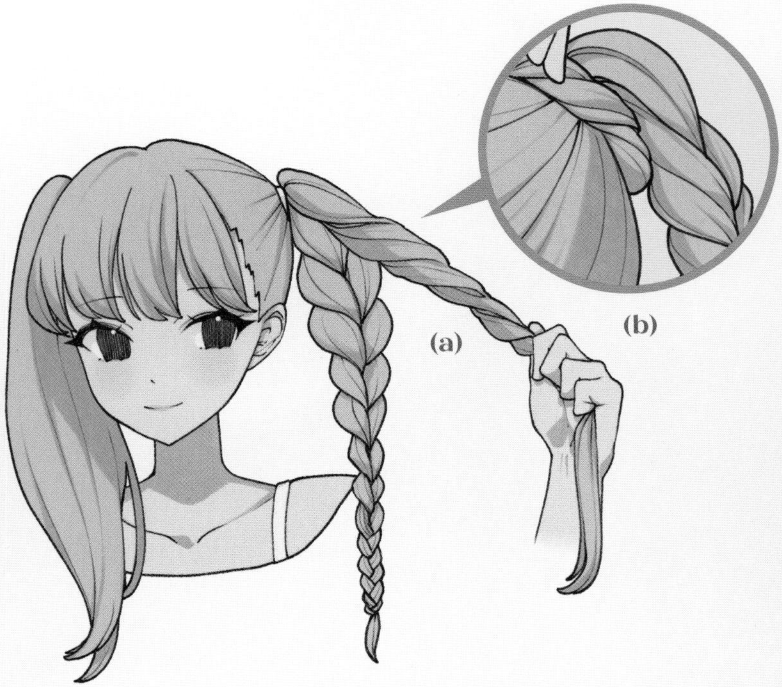
(a)
(b)

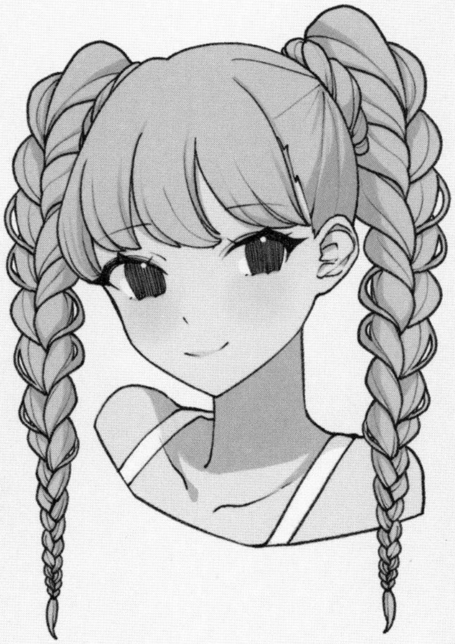

7 For the 2-inch piece of hair previously sectioned, tightly twist away from the face (a).

8 Wrap the twist around the base of the braid (b). Bobby pin in place and then gently loosen the twist for volume.

9 Lightly spray with hair spray to secure.

Konan

Naruto

Konan from *Naruto* is a fighter who uses origami as her weapon, the delicately folded paper rose in her hair reflecting her unusual power. To represent that concept, I decided to use my own hair as a medium to create a rose. As I've mentioned before in this book, my favorite solution for a lack of hair accessories is to make them myself!

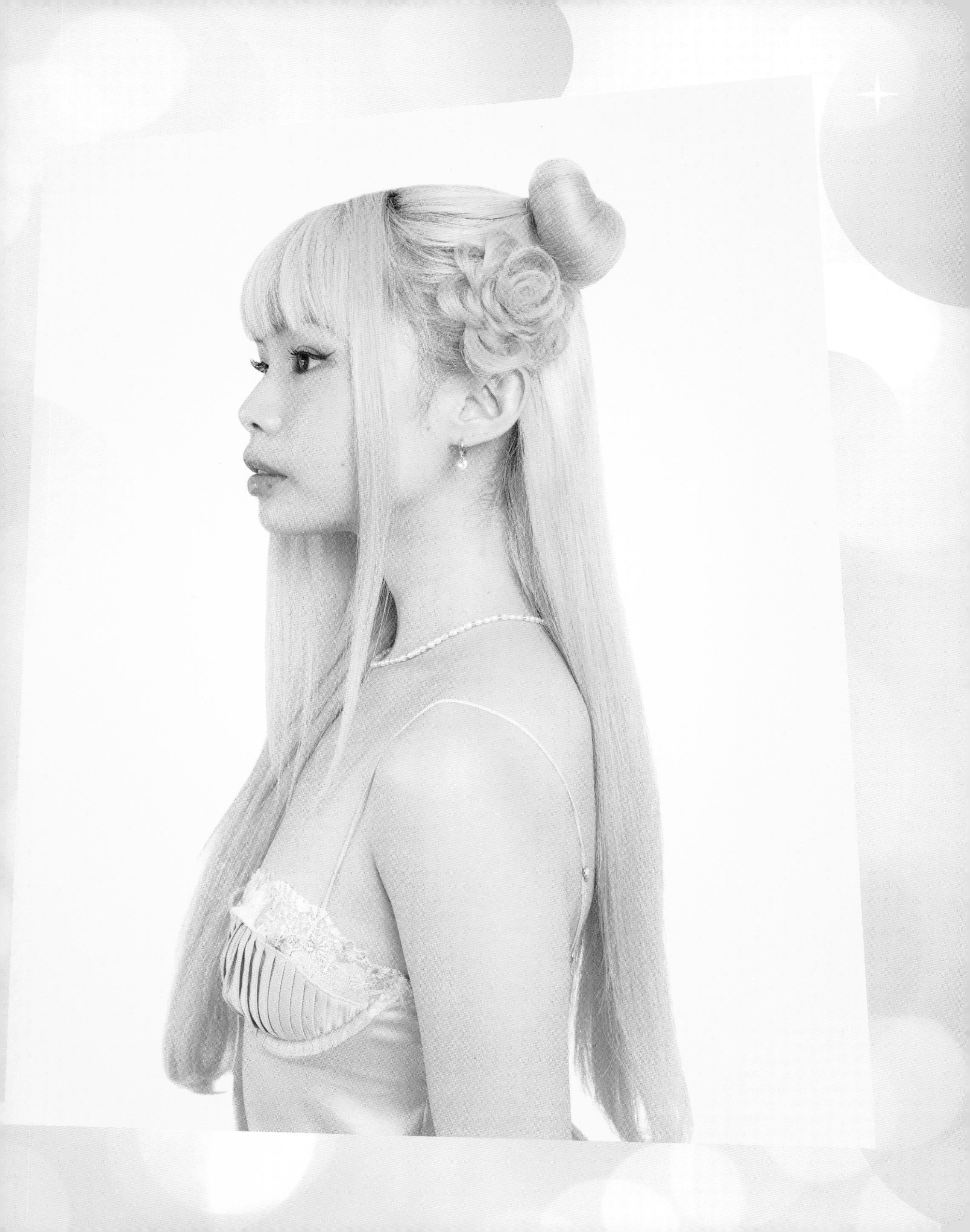

Tools

Elastics • Small bun maker • Bobby pins • Hair spray • Boar-bristle brush

1 Start with straight hair curled in at the bottom.

2 On the right side, gather the top half of the hair into a high pigtail, leaving out a 2-inch section of hair to frame the face. Secure with an elastic.

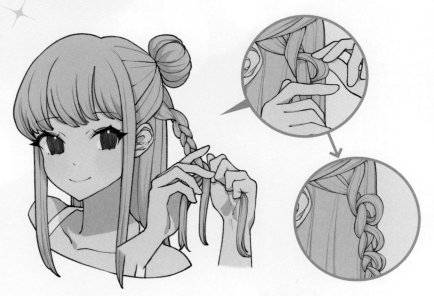

5 Begin making a three-strand braid, stopping every two braids to gently loosen one side of the braid. This will create the faux petals for the flower rose.

6 Continue to the end of the hair. Secure with an elastic.

3 Use a small bun maker to roll the pigtail into a bun and bobby pin in place.

4 Taking a 3-inch vertical section of hair above the ear, separate into three strands.

7 Roll the petal braid upward in a spiral to create the rose shape.

8 Gently bobby pin the rose above the ear.

9 Spray with hair spray to secure.

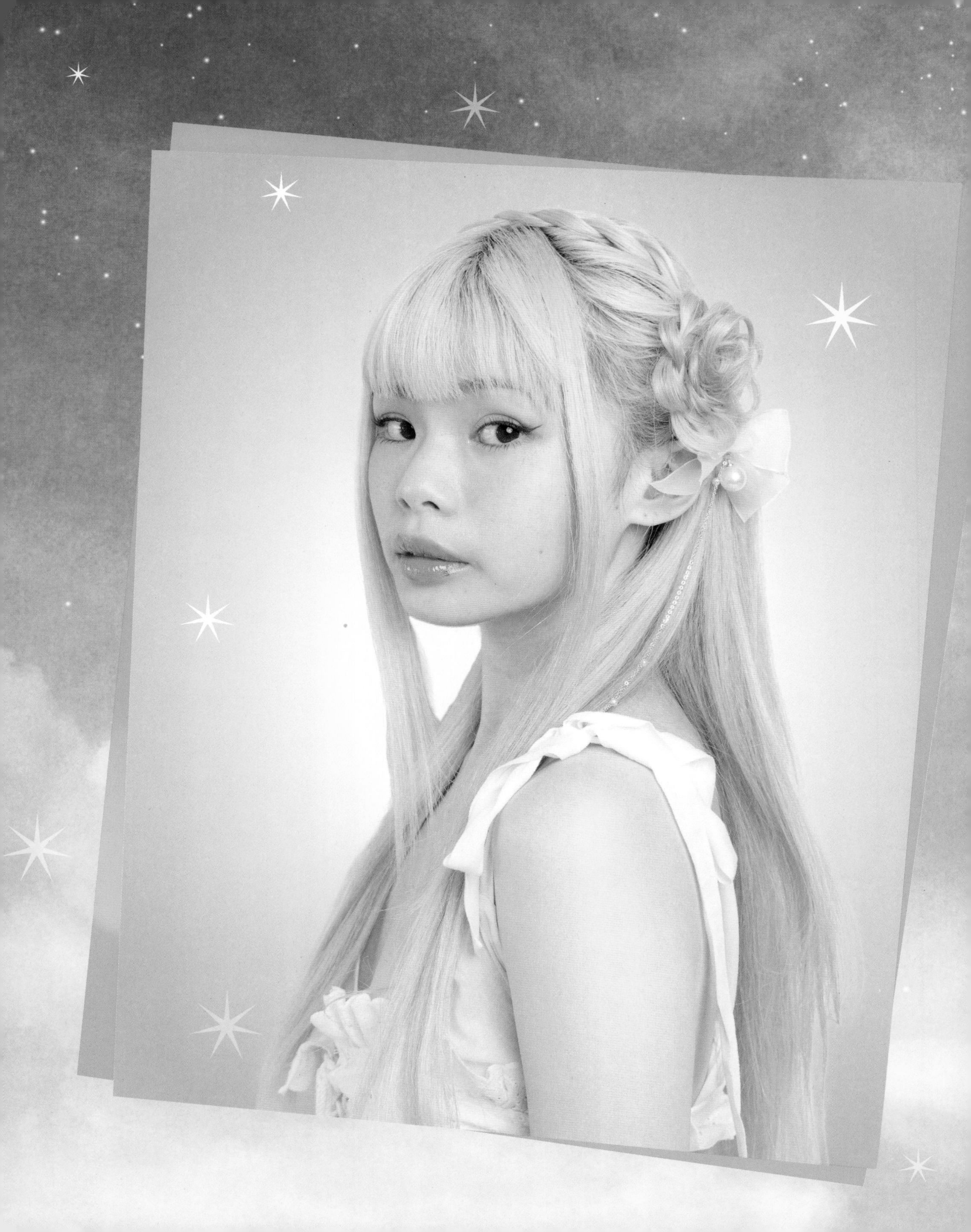

Emilia

Re:Zero

Now that you know how to create the perfect delicate rose (see the tutorial for Konan from *Naruto*, page 141), let's combine that with a second technique: a dainty braided hair crown. This is the perfect hairstyle for any special occasion because of the love, time, and effort that goes into the delicate parts. Wear it for a special date on a picnic, as a guest at a wedding, or for a photoshoot among blooming flowers.

Tools

Rat-tail comb • Elastics
• Bobby pins • Ribbon
hair clip • Hair spray

1 Start with straight hair with the ends curled in.

2 Using a rat-tail comb, section off a 2-inch section to frame the face. Create a side part 3 inches from the center of the head.

5 Section off a 3-inch section of hair from above the ear.

6 Create a petal braid (see the Konan from *Naruto* tutorial, page 142). Roll the petal braid upward in a spiral to create the rose shape and pin in place.

3 French-braid a 3-inch section of hair along the top of the head to create a braided crown.

4 Continue braiding with a three-strand braid until you reach the top of the ear on the opposite side of the head. Secure with an elastic.

7 Roll the petal braid upward in a spiral to create the rose shape and pin in place.

8 Accessorize with a ribbon hair clip beneath the rose to hide the elastic of the braided crown. Spray with hair spray to hold.

Yor Forger

Spy x Family ◆ Dark Version

We've covered Yor Forger's daily updo hairstyle earlier in this book, so now let's learn how to create the updo she wears for her Dark Version. Using the same rose hair technique from the Konan from *Naruto* tutorial (see page 141), we'll be creating the stunning hairstyle worn during her secret missions. This look goes to show that when you learn a technique once, you can utilize it in a million different ways to create any hairstyle your heart desires!

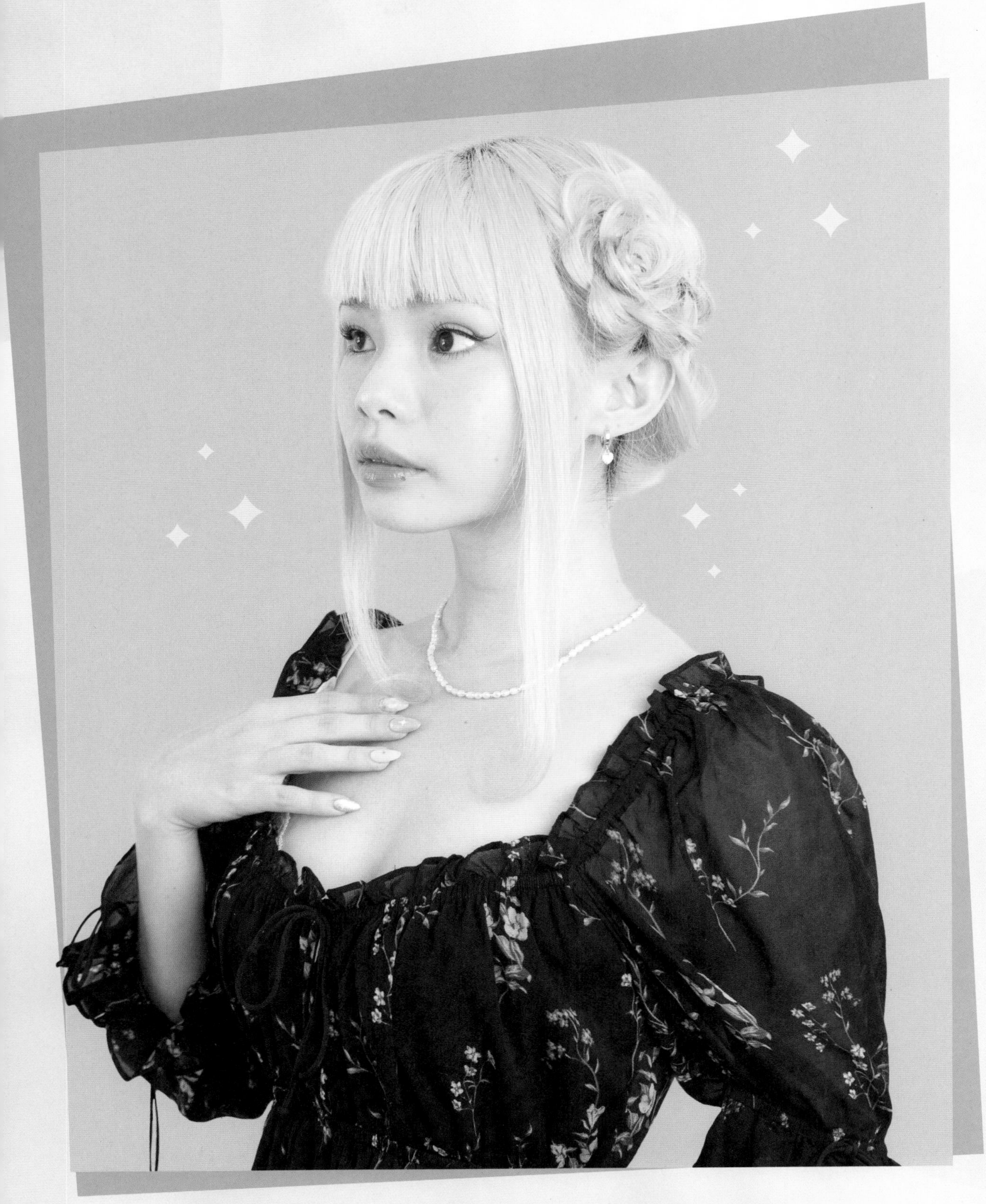

Tools

Rat-tail comb
• Elastics • Bobby pins
• Hair spray
• Headband (optional)

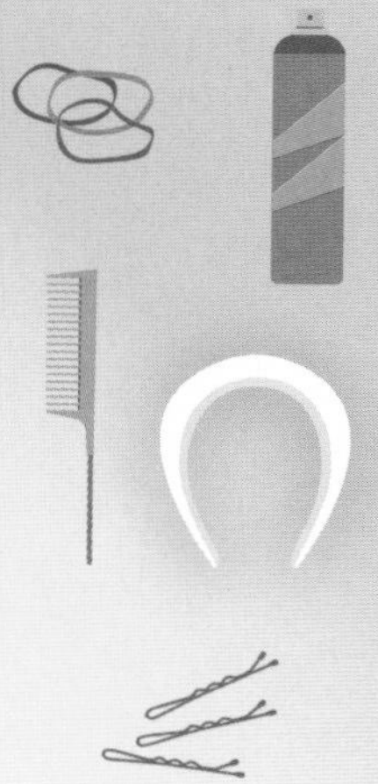

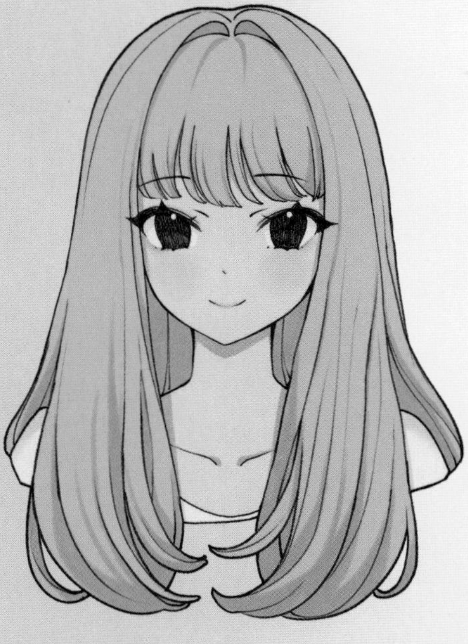

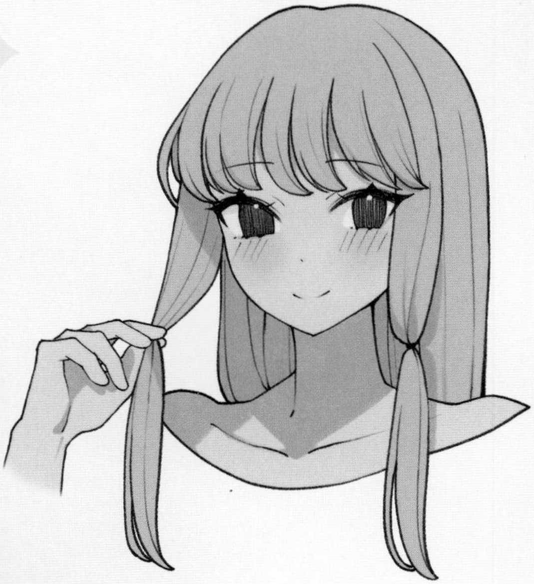

1 Start with straight hair with the ends curled in.

2 With a rat tail comb, separate a 3-inch section of hair in front of the ears on both side. Temporarily secure with an elastic to keep separate while working on the rest of the hairstyle.

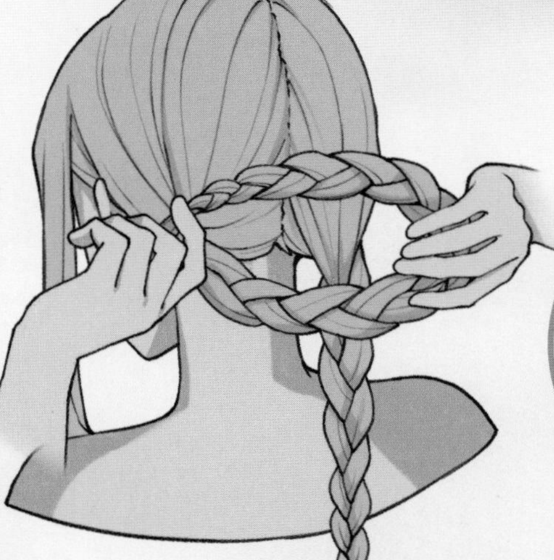

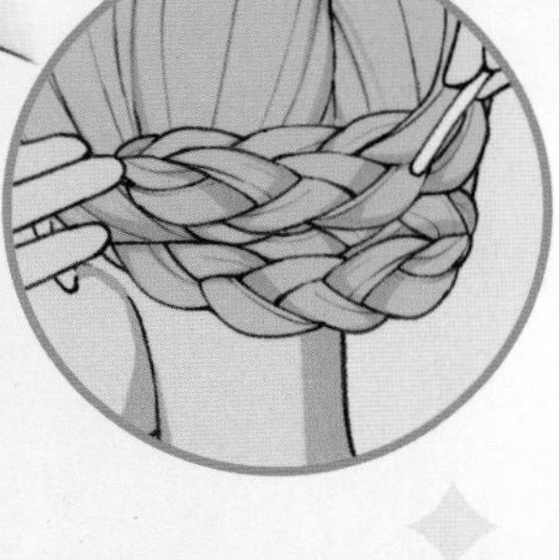

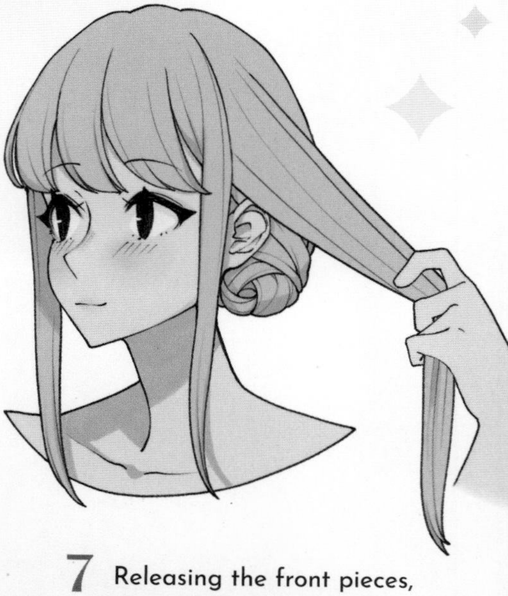

5 Following the same steps from the Yor Forger hairstyle (page 91) fold the left braid in half and lay across the head. Bobby pin in place.

6 Repeat on the other side for a low braided updo.

7 Releasing the front pieces, separate a 1-inch section from each side to frame the face.

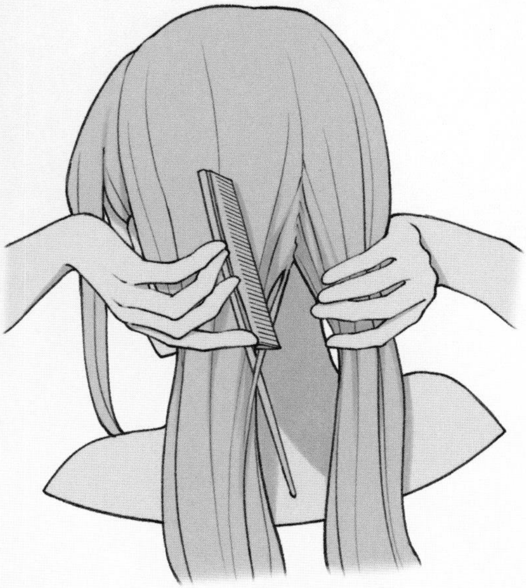

3 With a rat tail comb, separate the remaining hair straight down the center in the back.

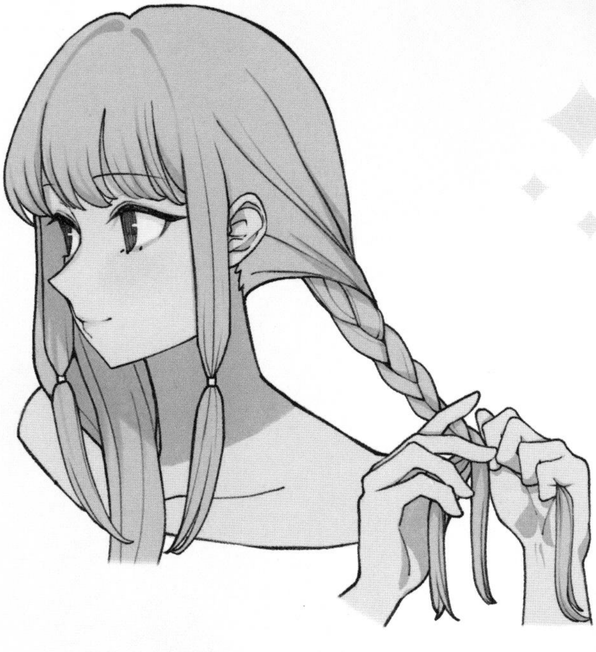

4 Create two three stranded braids on each sides and secure with an elastic.

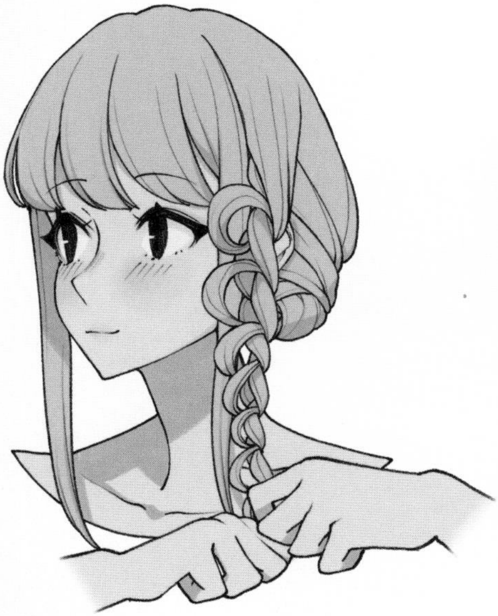

8 With the remaining 2-inch section of hair, follow the same steps from Konan (page 141) to create a three-strand braid with loops on one side.

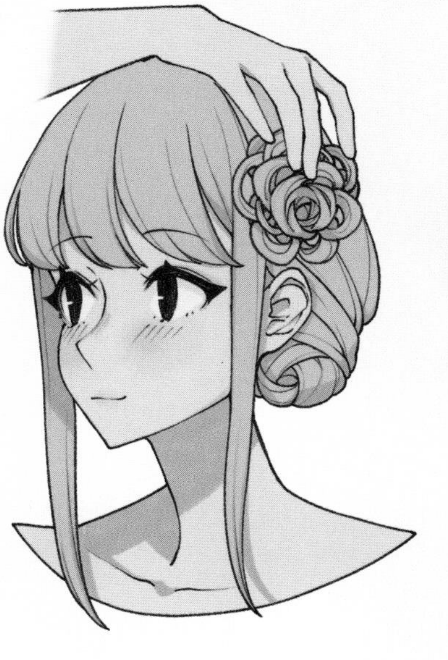

9 Starting from the end, roll the braid into a flower. Pin in place. Hair-spray to hold.

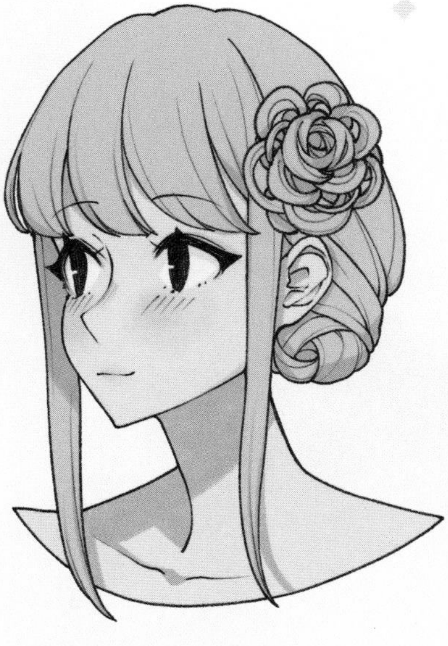

10 Repeat on the other side.

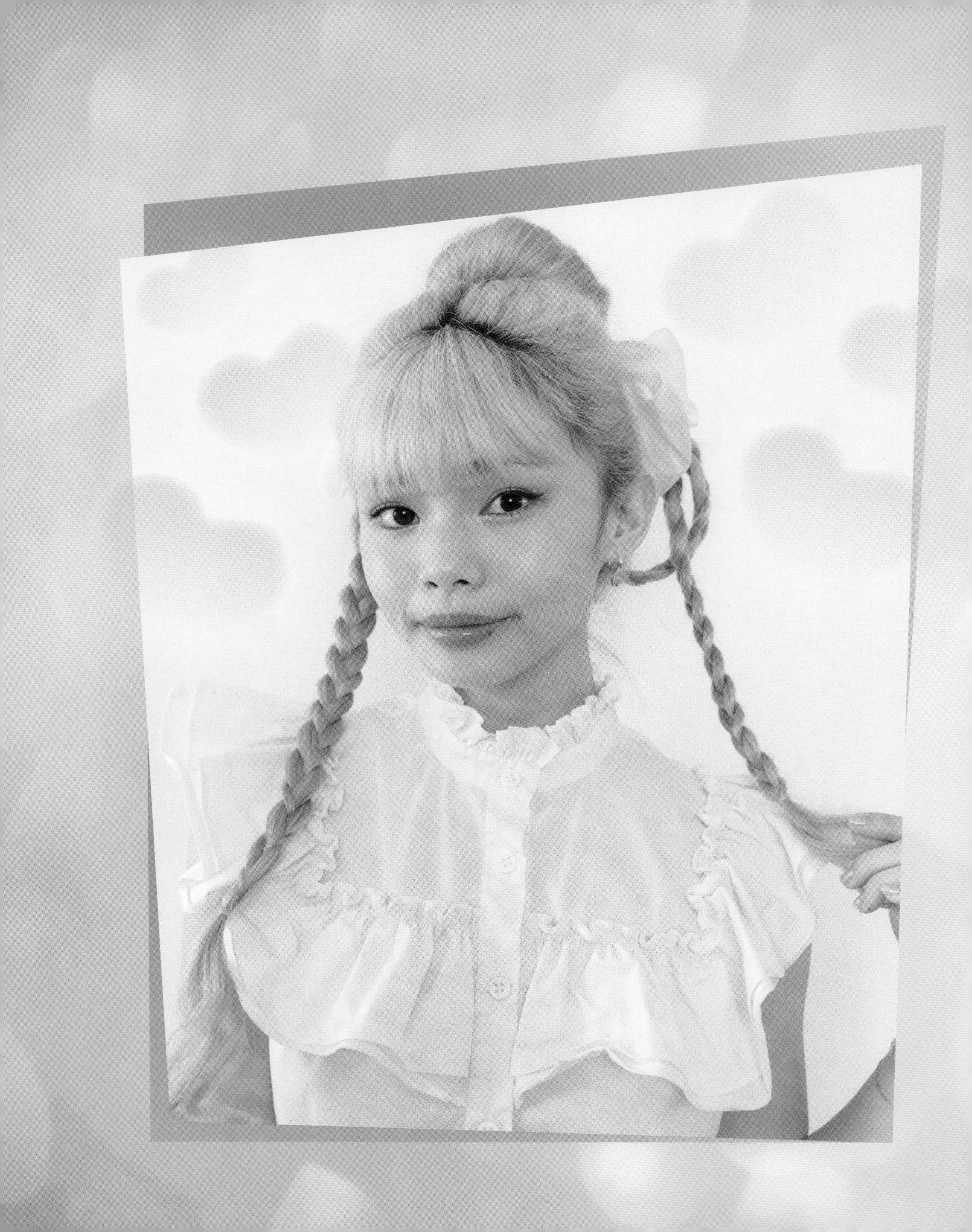

CereCere

Sailor Moon

At this point in the book, the techniques that you've learned should give you the ability to break down most anime hairstyles into several basic techniques at a glance. After that, all you have to do is figure out the steps in which to layer the techniques to create the final look.

Sailor CereCere is a lesser-known character in *Sailor Moon*, but her hair provides a fun and interesting challenge for those who want a unique look. Her hairstyle looks complicated, but once you take the time to break down the elements of it, you can see that this look is composed of one bun and four simple braids.

Tools

Bun maker • Bobby pins • Elastics • Curling iron • Large ribbon

1 Start with straight hair.

2 Gather the top third of hair to create a high ponytail. Secure with an elastic.

5 Split each pigtail in half to create two three-strand braids. There will be four braids in total.

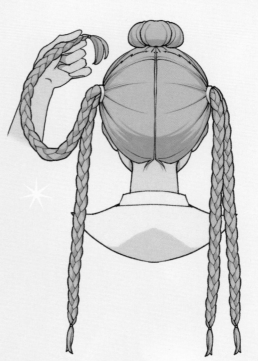

6 With the top braids from each pigtail, loop upwards towards the top of the bun and bobby pin in place.

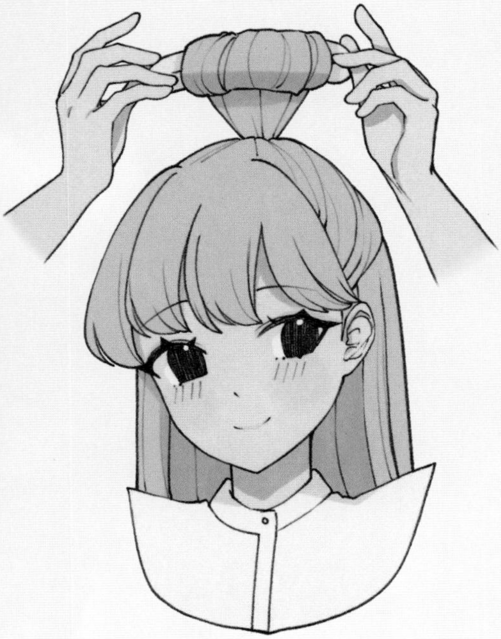

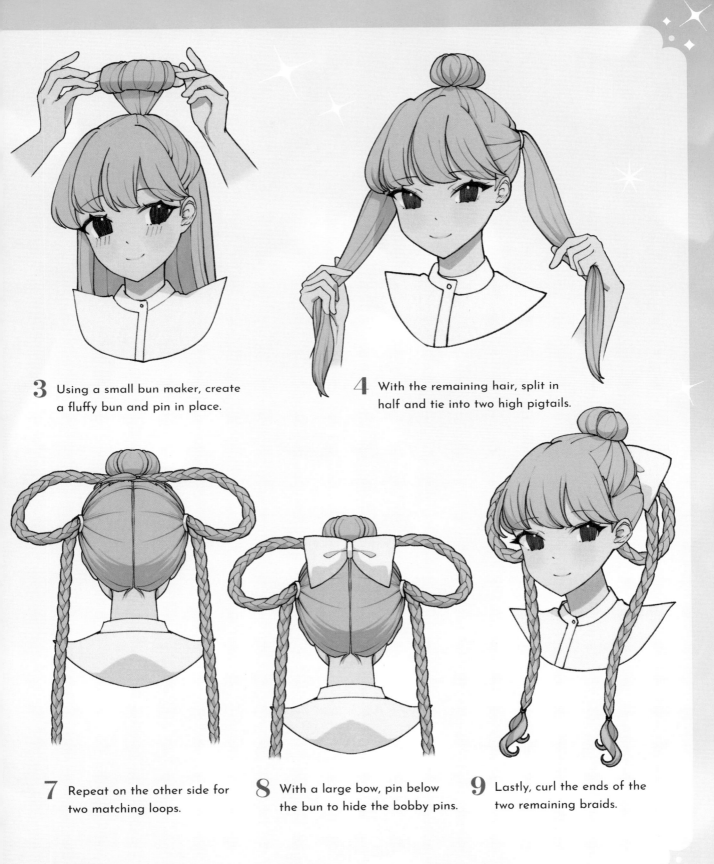

3 Using a small bun maker, create a fluffy bun and pin in place.

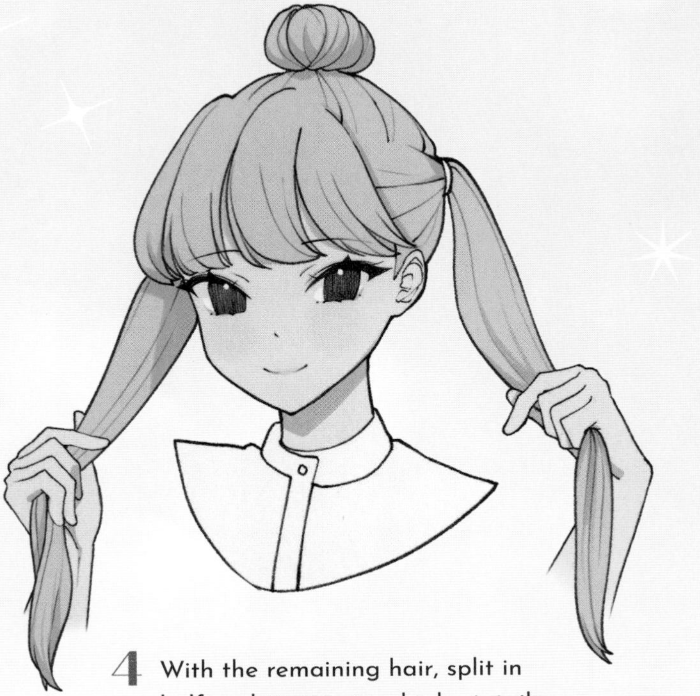

4 With the remaining hair, split in half and tie into two high pigtails.

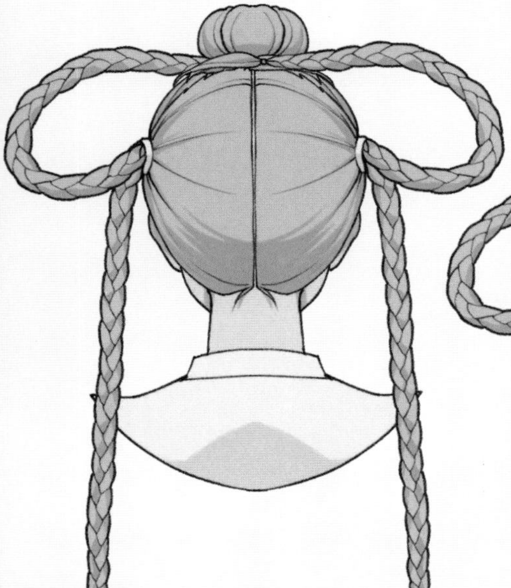

7 Repeat on the other side for two matching loops.

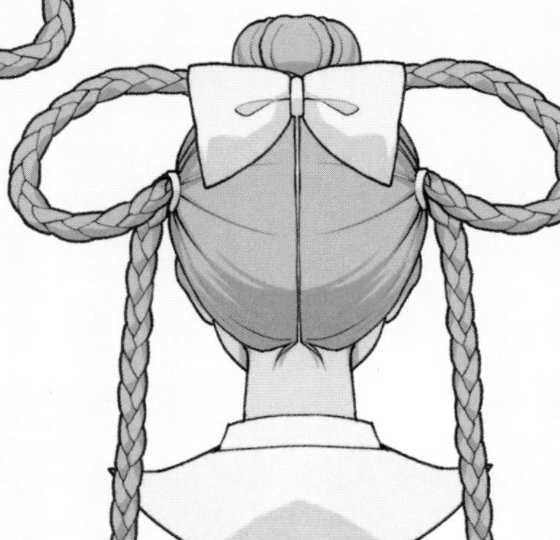

8 With a large bow, pin below the bun to hide the bobby pins.

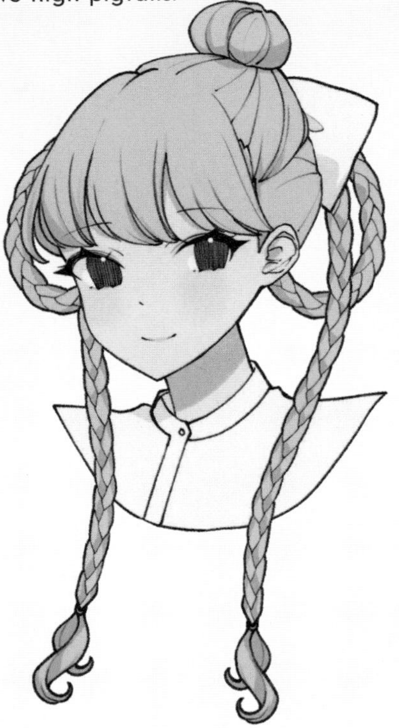

9 Lastly, curl the ends of the two remaining braids.

GLOSSARY OF HAIR TERMS

Hair extensions: Sections of real or synthetic hair that can be added to a look to create length, volume, or a pop of color. Hair extensions come in a multitude of styles with different installation processes. There are clip-ins, sew-ins, tape-ins, and glue-ins. For the purpose of easy installation and quick removal, we only use clip-in extensions in this book. Hair extensions also come in different materials of human hair, synthetic fiber, or a mix of the two. Because there are many different options on the market, I recommend doing research to decide what's right for you before purchasing a set.

A full set of hair extensions generally includes five to nine pieces of hair, ranging in width, length, and weight. Select your ideal set of hair extensions based on the weight and texture of your natural hair to have a seamless blend between the two.

Half updo: Half of the hair gathered upward into one or more parts.

Heat protection: A cream or spray-on product formulated to coat and protect the hair from heat damage during the use of hot styling tools.

Pigtail: Hair gathered into two parts and secured with elastics. Also known as twin tails in this book.

Ponytail: Hair gathered into one part and secured with an elastic.

Rat-tail comb: This is typically a plastic comb with a long metal stick on one end. The long stick helps neatly part hair into smaller sections, keeping your style symmetrical and tidy.

Types of Brushes:

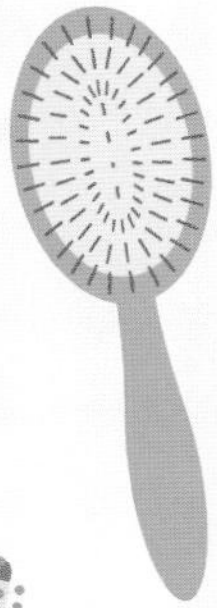

A **boar-bristle brush** can be made with authentic or synthetic boar bristles. The thick and stiff bristles help distribute hair spray, gel, and other hair products on the root of the hair to help smooth flyaways into place. This is especially helpful when creating sleek and tidy ponytails, pigtails, or updos.

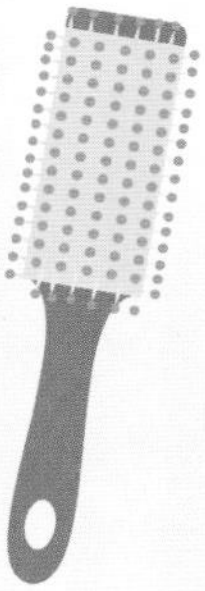

A **detangling hairbrush** is the perfect everyday hairbrush. Its soft and malleable bristles help detangle hair while reducing breakage and damage. It's highly recommended for helping maintain bleached or color-treated hair.

Types of Curls:

Loose curls are defined in this book as curls made by a 1½- to 2-inch-barrel curling iron.

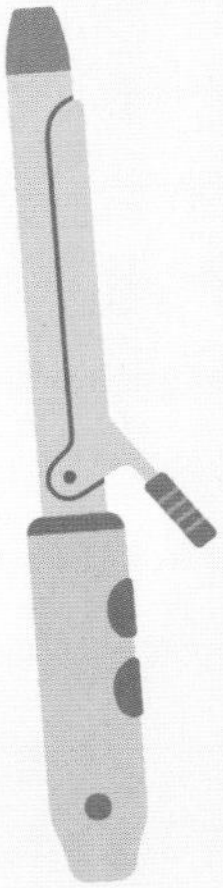

Rag curls are created by wrapping small sections of lightly damp hair around pieces of cloth and tying them into bundles before leaving overnight to dry. The method shown in this book to achieve this style is heatless.

Tight curls are defined in this book as curls made by a 1-inch-barrel curling iron. Also known as ringlets in this book.

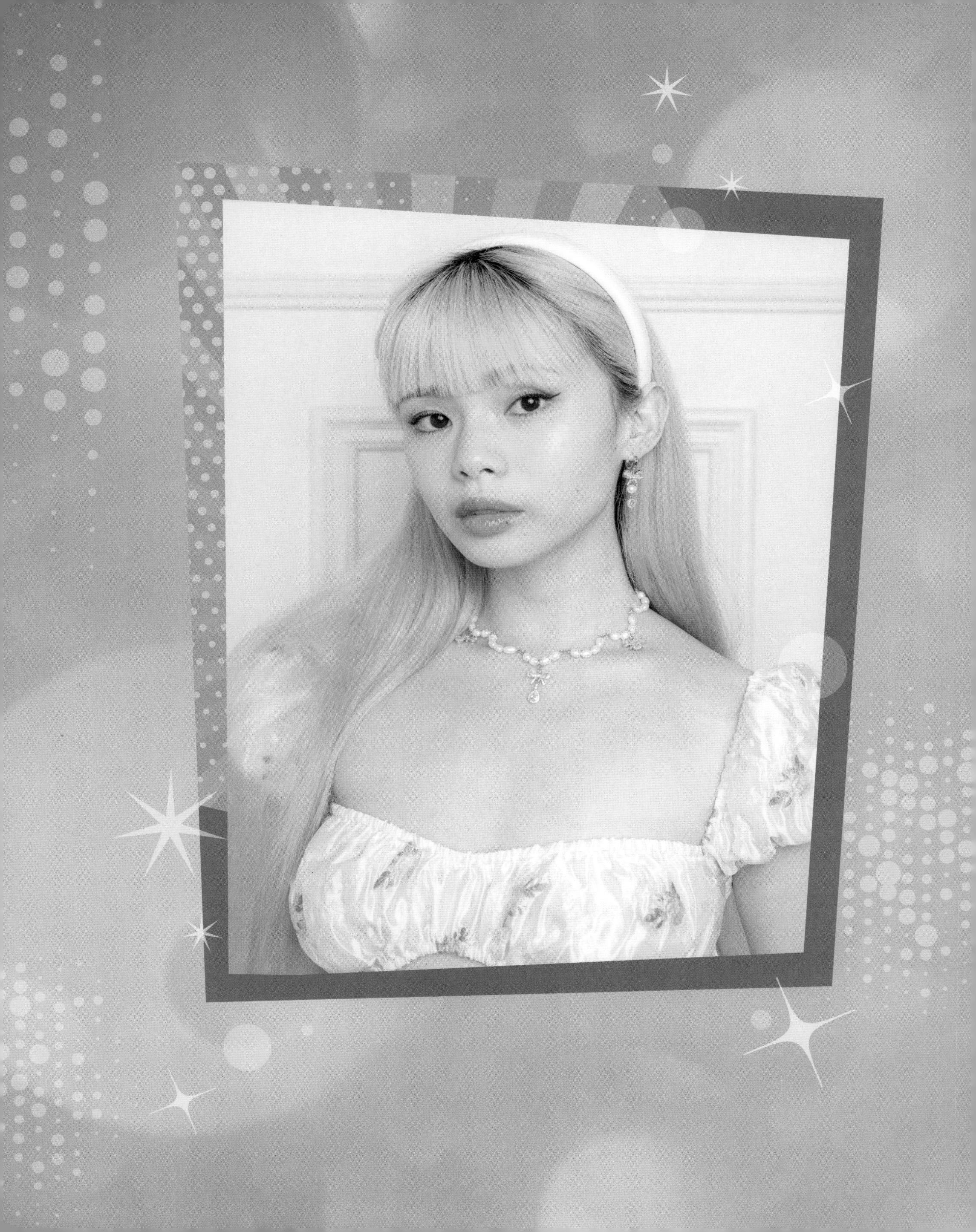

For my mom, who's always been my biggest fan.

ABOUT THE AUTHOR

Mei Yan is a Chinese American creator born and raised in Los Angeles, California. She started her career on YouTube and has amassed a following of almost one million fans across various platforms, with her most notable YouTube series recreating anime hairstyles. She's expanded her work past the digital world and now owns Meide, a jewelry brand featuring whimsical handmade jewelry.

© 2024 by Quarto Publishing Group USA Inc.
Photography © 2024 by May Yan

First published in 2024 by Epic Ink, an imprint of The Quarto Group,
142 West 36th Street, 4th Floor, New York, NY 10018, USA
(212) 779-4972 www.Quarto.com

All rights reserved. No part of this book may be reproduced in any form without written permission of the copyright owners. All images in this book have been reproduced with the knowledge and prior consent of the artists concerned, and no responsibility is accepted by producer, publisher, or printer for any infringement of copyright or otherwise, arising from the contents of this publication. Every effort has been made to ensure that credits accurately comply with information supplied. We apologize for any inaccuracies that may have occurred and will resolve inaccurate or missing information in a subsequent reprinting of the book.

Epic Ink titles are also available at discount for retail, wholesale, promotional, and bulk purchase. For details, contact the Special Sales Manager by email at specialsales@quarto.com or by mail at The Quarto Group, Attn: Special Sales Manager, 100 Cummings Center Suite 265D, Beverly, MA 01915 USA.

10 9 8 7 6 5 4 3 2 1

ISBN: 978-0-76038-553-1

Digital edition published in 2024
eISBN: 978-0-76038-554-8

Library of Congress Cataloging-in-Publication Data

Names: Yan, Mei, 1996- author.
Title: Dreamy anime hair : 30+ cute & easy styles from the world's most
   beloved anime characters / Mei Yan.
Description: New York, NY, USA : Quarto Publishing Group USA Inc., 2024. |
   Summary: "Try your hand at 35 anime-inspired hairstyles and give
   yourself the ultimate makeover with Dreamy Anime Hair"-- Provided by
   publisher.
Identifiers: LCCN 2023037543 (print) | LCCN 2023037544 (ebook) | ISBN
   9780760385531 (paperback) | ISBN 9780760385548 (ebook)
Subjects: LCSH: Hairstyles. | Comic strip characters--Japan.
Classification: LCC TT972 .Y29 2024 (print) | LCC TT972 (ebook) | DDC
   646.7/24--dc23/eng/20231215
LC record available at https://lccn.loc.gov/2023037543
LC ebook record available at https://lccn.loc.gov/2023037544

Group Publisher: Rage Kindelsperger
Editorial Director: Lori Burke
Creative Director: Laura Drew
Senior Art Director: Marisa Kwek
Managing Editor: Cara Donaldson
Editor: Katie McGuire
Cover and Step-by-Step Illustrations: Yoai
Interior Layout Design: Ashley Prine, Tandem Books

Printed in China

This publication has not been prepared, approved, or licensed by the author, producer, or owner of any motion picture, television program, book, game, blog, or other work referred to herein. This is not an official or licensed publication. We recognize further that some words, models' names, and designations mentioned herein are the property of the trademark holder. We use them for identification purposes only.